JOURNEY
TO THE
"PROMISED LAND"

JOURNEY
TO THE
"PROMISED LAND"

AUTHOR MORRIS LEWIS

XULON PRESS

Xulon Press
2301 Lucien Way #415
Maitland, FL 32751
407.339.4217
www.xulonpress.com

Unless otherwise indicated, Scripture quotations taken from the King James Version (KJV) – *public domain.*

Paperback ISBN-13: 978-1-6628-4110-1
Ebook ISBN-13: 978-1-6628-4111-8

Table of Contents

Preface of the book *Journey to the Promised Land* revised in 2020

Below is a copy of a personal letter sent to me from a sister in Christ, Billie Cheney, who read the original writing in 2013. After voting to sell the Promised Land, the first manuscript was given to some First Baptist Church of Immokalee members. The goal of this book was to change the hearts of those who voted to sell the Promised Land. This book focuses on why it was a mistake to sell the Church property. In addition, it focuses on the details and miracles that took place to make it possible for the Promised Land dream to come to a reality.

The *Journey to Promised Land* took over 100 years to complete. Your focus should be on the Journey. My Journey and your Journey. While reading this book, you should recognize that you experienced some of the same experiences in your own life. This book about the Journey is full of spiritual facts and miracles. It should inspire any believer and even non-believer to develop a personal relationship with Jesus. Each reader should see themselves in this Journey as they journey through life.

The overall tone encourages all believers that our Lord is always with us in our Life's JOURNEY. It will give the believer hope in this upside-down world that we live in today. We can do all things with his help as long as we are in his will. No matter who you are, God loves us, a believer or non-believer in Christ. He can use anyone willing to be used no matter how inadequate your talents you may believe you have. God is always present with the believer. He is also knocking on the heart of the nonbeliever.

We can do anything with his help. He is a good father who wants to give us peace and understanding of why things happen. All things do work together for good for those who love the Lord. As you read this book, with all the overtones themes and side streets, you should be encouraged to renew your mind of similar things that may have happened in your life. No matter how far we get from God, he is always there, waiting on us to return to him if we have gone astray. He is always willing to welcome home his prodigal sons and daughters.

This book is all about my life journey and the truths I have learned along my long journey. It is why I started with my personal history and the history of the church I attended. It should give the reader some insight into the author of this book. My personal history and the early history of the Church of Immokalee may be boring to some who read it. But I also believe that the reader may miss some insights into their own lives without reading it.

Other than my Lord, No other person has done more to encourage me to complete this book than Billie Cheney. In recent years, she and her family have gone through some very hard-to-understand events. I have read her letter to me repeatedly for many years, which continues to encourage me to finish the task my Lord has put into my mind, heart, and soul. I have also asked her to help me edit this book and give me her input. She is a great sister in Christ with lots of insight and wisdom. She also had a part, as many others did, in saving the Promised Land from destruction in 2013. Of all those I gave a copy of the original book written in 2013, she appreciated and supported the most. Every time I got discouraged in finishing this book, I read the letter below.

Thanks to Billie Cheney, who wrote the below letter to me, Morris Lewis.

Morris, I truly enjoyed your book. I started reading it last night and finished it today. I loved the reading of the church and how the build of the new Baptist church came about. It was inspiring to read of the love, commitment, and dedication from you and the others you mentioned in your book, as one would say, the blood, sweat, and tears of the faithful. It was so encouraging and uplifting to my soul.

I could feel the spiritual pain you went through during your life and the pain you went through as you went into your wilderness. I sensed the moving of the Holy Spirit in your life. Also, I could feel the genuine love and deep art-wrenching concern you had and still have for the church today.

Morris, God has a reason for your writing this book, and He has his hand on you!

Your sister in Christ Billie Cheney April 2013.

This is an illustrated picture of the facility, built on the Promised Land. After the buildings were finished and before the first Church service, the Miracle of the <u>Halo,</u> not a rainbow. It covers the entire building for many hours. It was as it was a statement for God, "Well done, thou Good and Faithfull servants."

This picture Illustrates where my family and I were picking up trash, where suddenly a Halo over the entire Church building appeared the day before the first church service.

Front Entrance into the Church Sanctuary and the doors were the Miracles of Carol Ford the Rock mason appeared opened and came into the foyer. Another one of the many miracles written about in the book.

Introduction

JOURNEY to the "Promised Land"

It is a book about the physical and spiritual **Miracles** that happen while we are on our **Journey** to the **Promised Land**. It focuses on the Miracles that occurred before and while building the First Baptist Church of Immokalee in the 1980s.

This story is about the **Journey** and also about real, touchable, seeable Miracles. A life's **Journey** of 100 years it took to reach the Promised Land. A book about my Journey and the Miracles helped me accomplish a task that My Lord wanted to complete for his glory. This book is based upon real-life, touchable experiences that we could see, feel, touch, witness, and understand. It should encourage you to believe in Miracles and recognize that you had some in your own life.

As I share this **journey** with you in this book, it is hoped that you will realize that God was and is always in control. Although many times, when we are on our life's **JOURNEY**, we may not or do not understand why certain things happened to us. Only after reflection of our entire life's **JOURNEY** and looking backward at the total picture of our life's journey,

7

both the good, bad, happy, sad experiences, can we begin to understand that God has always been there with ME and YOU.

Hopefully, this book will give you an understanding of your <u>Journey</u> through life and insight into how different events were not by accident, both the good and bad events which molded us by divine intervention, preparing us for our future calling. These events usually can only be understood as we reflect in our own lives how God arranged specific concrete path changes in our life so we would be in a position to honor him and carry on his perfect plan.

> *Romans 8:28. We know that all things work together for good to them that love God, to them who are called according to his purpose.*

It is hoped while reading this book that you will reflect in your mind about your own personal life's Journey. Hopefully, you will understand after looking back that events just did not happen to you by accident. Hopefully, you will recognize that God created the roadways or paths in your journey in life. Of course, it is your choice to choose which way you shall travel down in your life's journey.

> *Romans 7 18 <u>For</u> I <u>know</u> <u>that</u> <u>in</u> <u>me</u> (that <u>is</u>, <u>in</u> <u>my</u> flesh,) <u>dwelleth</u> <u>no</u> good <u>thing</u>: <u>for to</u> <u>will is</u> <u>present</u> with <u>me</u>, <u>but</u> how to <u>perform</u> that which is <u>good</u> I <u>find</u> <u>not</u>.*

But I believe it even goes further than that. We do not recognize these events at the time they are happening. God causes certain circumstances in your life's journey that encouraged you or caused you to travel down the roads/paths that we did. Bad things can work for good for those who love the Lord and are called for his purpose. I believe before you accept Jesus, the Lord was working in our lives. Just take a few moments to clear your mind in a quiet personal space and reflect in your own life how God has been with you in your entire journey through life. God will speak to your heart and mind to remind you.

This book is written primarily to the believer, but it also should be helpful to the nonbeliever. The Miracles that happen in my Journey are tangible, touchable, experienced, and witnessed by others. If you compare them to the miracles that happened in Biblical times, they are relatively recent events. I believe Miracles are happening all around us today that we fail to recognize.

However, our lack of faith has blocked us from seeing them. When they happen, we are too busy or worried about our situation and are blinded and cannot see them. Take a few moments and reflect in your own life on the times and events that occur to you that you cannot explain in your mind why they happen.

Today, I believe God has been laying on more hearts to write more about the Miracles they have personally experienced in their personal lives. Maybe you have noticed that fact in different books and even movies. I wonder if our God is getting humanity prepared for the Miracle of his second coming. I believe the time of the tribulation is close at hand. It could be beneficial to those who read about or see the many different miracles God has done. Maybe if some could read a book or see a movie about God's Miracles, it would help them get through this terrible time in history.

I do not know, but one thing I can say for sure is in my personal life as I have struggled through life's JOURNEY and many difficult times that the MIRACLES that I experienced helped me get through them. So many times when I believed there was no hope, my Lord reminded me of a MIRACLE I had witnessed in my past, which gave me the faith and strength to continue the race and hopefully finish the course that he had laid out before me.

Some pastors tell believers that the Christian experience will be full of milk and honey. Christians feel suitable for a while, but when the first sign of something negative happens to them, they fold and run for the hills. Unfortunately, the Bible is full of bad things happening to those who love the Lord the most. Paul, Peter, Job, and David are a few of the hundreds of examples.

There can be no other explanation or description for many special advents written about in this book except MIRACLE. Miracles and the Christian journey started many years ago. But this recent journey actual factual event began in 1913. It should be proof of the non-believe that God still does exist today. That he still cares about you and still is involved in our everyday lives. God is real and alive. He does love you no matter what sin you have committed. He will forgive you, and he will save you.

Romans 5:8: But God commendeth his love toward us, in that, while were yet sinners, Christ died for us.

This book should encourage believers and nonbelievers to believe the Bible's words are true, accurate, and factual. This book is based on facts and not fiction; it should help every believer there is one God and only one God. The reason I know this is I have experienced them. The MIRACLES I experienced have proven this to me without any doubt. Therefore, there is a God and that he loves me, and he will guide our path if you let him.

I believe it is essential to establish another fact at this point. Understanding that many do not believe the Bible is factual and accurate. The Bible is the inspired Word of God. After many years of studying God's Word, I have never found any contradictions or any reason not to believe every detail written in it. I know the most brilliant people I know, Doctors, teachers, lawyers, and engineers, all think there is a God. Even the demons believe that there is a God.

James 2:19: Thou believest that there is one God, thou doest well. The demons also believe and tremble

All of us live on Earth, and if we take time to think about nature and its wonder, we have to know that God created it. It was not created by accident, as some have said. Nature itself scrams out there is a God. Just take a look at the sky in the daytime and also at the stars at night. Study the human body and how it functions. There has to be something that caused/created the universe.

> *Romans 1:20: For the invisible things of him from the creation of the world are seen, being understood by the things, that are made, even His eternal power and Godhead, so that they are without excuse*

Some have said that the Big Bang Theory created the world, others by other methods. But when you examine what they are saying, it is easier to believe there is a God than those theories. Some say that the earth could not have been created in 7 days, as the book of Genesis teaches. Although I believe that my God has all power and can do anything, he wants instantly. There are insights in the Bible that <u>may</u> explain the timing of creation.

> *2 Peter 3:8: But beloved is not ignorant of this one thing that one day with the Lord as thousand years, and a thousand years as one day.*

This verse means to me that God even controls time itself.

I know that all the predictions in the Bible have already or are coming to the past as predicted. How could these predictions made 2000 years ago be foreseen and written? This fact makes me believe every word in the Bible is factual and accurate. We may not understand it yet, but it will all be revealed to us one day.

Let me encourage you to read the predictions/prophecy in the Bible. All have been proven true or are going to become true in the future. So when you read the scriptures verses I have included in the book, accept them as accurate and factual. I could write about many Prophecies that would strengthen your faith. But I am only going to include a few in this book. One of the most recent prophecies was revealed in 2020.

Revelation 14:17: And that no man might buy or sell, except he that had the mark or the name of the beast, or the number of his name. 20:4: ...had received his mark upon their foreheads, or their hands

We are all aware of the computer chips which have been on our credit cards for a few years now. But, did you know that the Bible predicted 1000s years ago that those living in the last days would have a number on their forehead or the palm of their hands? It was hard to imagine how this could be years ago, but today everyone knows about computer chips. Computer chips can be inserted into animals to be tracked and located when lost.

In recent days in 2020 and 2021, there has been a worldwide Covid-19 plague on the entire world. We must take a vaccination card with us to board airplanes and cruise ships. Some businesses need us to show them before we can enter their businesses. We also have bar codes that when we check out almost all companies. Some want to get rid of all the cash transactions. They only want credit or debit cards to be used to buy or sell.

It seems as if all governments in every country are trying to control their population.

With the wave of a tool, these chips or bar codes can instantly let businesses know the price and the items you may be purchasing. All most of us do is put our credit card chip into a machine, and bam, we have the funds to buy items. It is not unreasonable to assume that we may not buy or sell without preapproval by using these new systems. Could it happen soon that you may not buy or sell if you do not have this chip/ number/bar code? It could also tell someone; the Government/ a computer, I call it the beast, everything about you. Most of our phones already track our movements and know where we are at all times. Can you imagine living today without a CC or a cell phone. Could this be gradually conditioning our minds and hearts to accept the numbers, chips, bar codes, etc., as Revelation 14:17 predicts? Then, the one-world government in our future would be able to control everyone as the Bible has predicted.

Matthew 17-20:20 He replied, "Because you have so little faith. Truly I tell you, if you have faith as small as a mustard seed, you can say to this mountain, 'Move from here to there,' and it will move. Nothing will be impossible for you.

I believe, in fact, (know that) I was called to do this specific task. And also that my Lord had been preparing me for my entire life's journey. Thinking back, I can also understand how my Lord had been directing others' paths to reach the same goal, even though they were traveling down different journeys than I was.

I believe God let me experience/witness these Miracles in my life's journey and the actual physical Miracles that happen from the facility's building and reaching the Promised Land to increase my faith. Very similar as Jesus did when he worked the Miracles that his disciples witnessed and wrote about. One of the reasons they were so faithful was that they witnessed the Miracles. As a result, they had faith and could see, experience, and touch many of the Miracles that Jesus performed.

In the path of life's journey and in the process of fighting off Satan's firry darts during the idea, the conception of a new Church facility, until the completion of the facility, my Lord kept pouring out his recognizable, touchable Miracles. Thus, my spirit was renewed when seemly insurmountable, impossible obstacles would come up in the long process of reaching the Promised Land. It is very similar to when Mosses led the Children of Israel before going to their Promised Land. God performed many miracles to see, feel, and touch so they would not lose their faith in their JOURNEY TO THE PROMISED LAND.

These Miracles gave me factual proof that I witnessed, experienced, could grab hold of, and touched. Even today, when

I get down in the dumps, depressed about world events, dealing with family problems, and so much more, I still reflect on the physical, touchable, factual, Miracles that I and others experienced in building the physical facility of the First Baptist Church of Immokalee. Remembering these Miracles and my JOURNEY to the PROMISED LAND still gives me strength today to face the many troubles of life. If you recognize the Miracles God has done in your personal life, it will do the same for you

> *Philippians 4:13: I can do all things through Christ, which strengtheneth me.*

These Miracles give me the tangible, present-day reminders that my Lord is still in control. If he did it in my past, he is still with me today. As the Bible states, he will never leave or forsake us.

> *Heb 13:5 Let your conversation be without covetousness and be content with such things as ye have for he hath said, I will never leave thee nor forsake thee.*

The Miracles in the Bible, I believe they are all true. But there is a vast difference between just reading about the Miracles and real-life experiencing them for me and maybe you. All the Miracles mentioned in the book are REAL; I experienced them. I have seen them. Lord, forgive me for my lack of faith. A real personal experienced Miracle has more meaning than the one I have read out of the Bible. May God continue to bless those who believe only through faith, not requiring anything else but faith!

2 Co 5:7 For we walk by faith, not by sight.

I also believe if you will look back and reflect. Every Christian could examine their own life's Journey and rediscover a moment in their life that can not be explained except by using the word Miracle.

The dictionary describes a Miracle as:

"An extraordinary occurrence that surpasses all known human powers or natural forces and is ascribed to a divine or supernatural cause." 2 a superb or surpassing example of something, wonder or marvel.

I believe that you should latch on to, hold on to those advents, the Miracles, which will give you more faith in dealing with trouble, problems, disappointments, failures, heartache, and much more.

I also believe the worse is yet to come since we live in the last days as Revelation's book is becoming more understood as God reveals it to us.

If you would reflect and examine your own life, especially if you are a believer, the Lord will reveal Miracles in your own personal life's Journey, which should increase your faith. You should build your confidence in a solid foundation like a rock.

This true story is about the Journey and Miracles that happen to First Baptist Church of Immokalee. Give the Lord all the praise and credit for the events over 100 years. The Lord put events in a definite order to complete his Church Building on Hwy 29 and Lake Trafford Rd in Immokalee, Florida, in 1987. However, it is not the whole story because the Promised Land after it was taken was in danger of being destroyed and lost forever in 2013.

This book was not written to give anyone credit or praise. But some do deserve to be remembered, honored, and respected. After reading this history, it should be clear to anyone reading it that the Lord was involved in getting his church built over many years. Only by his will and miracles was the Church Building completed. The Lord used real-life and practical experiences to prepare and guide many for the task he set before them through their walk in life.

Morris Lewis does not take any credit for doing anything. I believe that I was the most unlikely person to be chosen to lead, similar to the story about Mosses. Of course, I am not any Mosses, but the Lord takes pleasure in choosing the most unlikely person to do his work. I get into this in more detail later in this book. However, I am still amazed at how the Lord did it and the many miracles that my Lord had to put into place in a definite order to make his Church building a reality.

The Lord has lain upon my heart to write what happened during our **JOURNEY TO** and the **MIRACLES that occurred while we were on our JOURNEY**.

At first, I believed the Lord only led me to write this true story because at the first writing that some were considering selling the First Baptist Church building located on

Highway 29 and Lake Trafford rd. These events were going on in 2013 in the First Baptist Church of Immokalee. This book was written then and was used to help save the First Baptist Church of Immokalee from being destroyed by Satan. The manuscript, written in 2013, was given to several of the leaders to motivate them to stand up and save the Church location and facility, **THE PROMISED LAND**.

I call the First Baptist Church of Immokalee at the corner of Lake Trafford and highway 29, **THE PROMISED LAND**. It is the name that a past pastor, Bother Babb Adams, named it. After a detailed discussion with him, I researched the history of how the land was purchased and learned many other details. I write about this in much greater detail later in this book. History creates a foundation to build on.

I believe it will help the reader better understand the Journey and the Miracles if they know some History. Brother Adams compared the Journey and Miracles to the Journey and the Miracles that the Children of Israel experienced in their Journey to their Promised Land. It is a beautiful part of the Bible that should be read and understood. My Journey also includes a parallel story to the 10 of 12 spies who said that the Promised Land could not be taken. In our case could not be built.

Numbers: all of Ch 13: 1-33 V 1: And the Lord spoke to Moses, saying. 2 Send thou men, that they may search the land of Canaan, with I give unto the children (12 Spies)

V 33: And there we saw the giants, the sons of Anak, who come of the giants; we were in our sight as a grasshopper, and so we were in the sight.

Numbers Ch 14: v 2: And all the children of Israel murmured against Moses against Aaron, and the whole congregation said unto them. Would God that we had died in the land of Egypt. Or would God we had died in this wilderness.

The first writing was to encourage, renew, and build up the faith of the members of the Church in Immokalee. Who was going through a very uncertain time concerning the continuation of their Church facility and the <u>PROMISED LAND</u>? It was written to remind them of the church's history, journey, and background in building the Promised Land facility.

There also may be other Churches considering a building or dealing with similar issues that our church family had to deal with in this true story. This book may help them so they will understand the battle that is before them.

This book must be accepted and read like a true story. The reader should believe that Miracles are real. They did happen. This revised edition, 2020, has blended in both the past and future importance and insight into how our Lord works in our daily lives. It is a blending of the past, present, and future.

I believe the Lord has again touched my mind and soul to write this revision and is far more critical considering the world we live in today, dealing with COVID-19, world events, and uncertainty in ours. The truth is this book will help all believers and increase their faith. It will help them recognize how God is with us and walk by our side every day as we journey through life.

The book of Revelation is still a mystery, but we are gaining more insight into it because of recent events. We can finally understand how today's events are possible as predicted 1000s of years ago. Thus, the book of Revelation is being revealed to us as we experience new insight into our current world events.

It may be hard for those who read this book to follow this story because of the back and forth. However, it examines both past and events. Keep in mind that this book started close to 100 years ago. Therefore, the reader can comprehend how the Lord works over time. Hopefully, once you grasp this concept, you will look back at your own life. Thus, recognizing how the Lord has been working in our own lives for many years.

It is also essential that readers grasp the real-life, accurate, touch, and see Miracles on the Journey to the Promised Land. Accepting this book's facts as accurate will give hope and strength to all those of little faith. I, Morris Lewis, confidently state that all the Miracles that happen on this long journey to the Promised Land are real. I witnessed them. Some were only between my Lord and me. Others also witnessed them.

These were touched, felt, and experienced Miracles, not just words of hope or inspiration.

Understanding the complete history of history over 80-100 is very important, especially today. This book points out how our Lord works over time, as the Bible's actual history, to get the job done that he has put into place. But these are current events, not 4000 years ago, BC or AC.

This book contains many <u>Side Streets,</u> as I call them. As I write this book, I know that my Lord sent me down these side streets to help the First Baptist Church members in 2013. But, even more important, it should increase and strengthen the faith of all who read it. This book is for every Christian. It should also reach the unbeliever, touch their heart and soul, and encourage them to become believers in Jesus.

I believe that the many <u>side streets</u> traveled down during this true story will help Christians'. It should give them a better understanding of Church family life and how <u>I believe</u> our Lord works in the daily lives of those who love him. These events have been recognized from hindsight, looking back on how the Lord used real-life experiences to achieve his goals. Others will have to write about their personal experiences. My life's journey will encourage joy, faith, courage, and purpose for believers and unbelievers.

They should give readers an understanding and recognize how the Lord works in our personal lives daily, as I share how the Lord worked in my life and others. This long <u>journey</u> over many years will witness how my Lord leads and guides our daily walk through life with him. Hopefully, by reading this book, the reader will gain insight into their walk with their Lord and, in hindsight, strengthen their faith.

It is a true story about how the Lord guided me and caused certain things to happen to me throughout my <u>life: JOURNEY</u> and others. Some experiences were good, some bad, and some were terrible. This book should give the reader an understanding that the Lord uses both the good and the bad to reach his final goal. But in the end, "All things work for Good"

I believe I was compelled to write this book so the Church members in 2013 could understand why the church building and location are essential. Brother Babb Adams and I thought it was a unique Holly Ground, set aside by God in his wisdom. They needed to be reminded and understand the Church Building's history and understand the sacrifices that so many made to build a reality. They needed to realize that these events did not just happen but were guided by God so that his church would be built on the PROMISED LAND.

I believe, and Brother Adams thought that just like the children of Israel when they were given by God the Promised Land, it was forever. Therefore, their Promised Land should never be abandoned. On the contrary, it will never be taken over or destroyed by the enemy Satan.

The Church/Flock/Shepard needed to be reminded of the many miracles that had to occur to build the faculty, the Promised Land. At the time of this book's original writing in, 2013 they were considering selling the Church property, the Promised Land.

They had forgotten that past pastors had told them many times; God ordained this special place. That God had said to them that he wanted his church built in this unique location. Most did not know or were not concerned about the history of the Promised Land. As a result, most had lost their faith. They had forgotten that "All things are possible with the Lord," no matter the present situation.

I believe that once they were reminded of their history and experienced the Miracles, they would change their minds about selling the Promised Land. I thought that a small raiment of believers would take a stand, stop, and revisit the vote to sell the Promised Land. Then, those who did not know the real story and history of how the Promised Land came to be would understand that the property should never be sold.

I also hoped that the church members of 2013 would understand that the vote to sell the Property in an unannounced, therefore, illegally called a business meeting in my opinion based upon their Church constitution would change their minds. The fact that only 23 members, out of membership on the Church rolls of over 200, voted to sell the Church building in 2013 was not correct nor what my Lord wanted.

It was this factual event that the Lord inspired me and compelled me to write this book. <u>The Lord had used me in a great way to understand his plan and also used me to build the new facility in 1985</u>. Therefore, I am probably the only person who knows the entire history and story.

My walk in the wilderness.

I was not living in Immokalee when the church voted to sell the Promised Land. I was angry with my Lord for almost 20 years. I blamed him for letting many bad things happen to me 20 years earlier. Living 250 miles away, I was not aware of the troubles in the church at that time.

In my mind did not believe the Lord had spoken to me from 1995-2013. However, that was not true. He had spoken to me many times, but I could not hear him because I blamed him for what had happened to me in a complete business failure. I finally realized that I was right where he wanted me to be. I finally realized that I was living a dream life in the Fl. Keys.

I lost my 6000 square foot home on 10 acres in Immokalee, now living in a 1000 square foot home in the Fl Keys. I lost my very successful businesses and was limited to a one-person business. I separated myself from God, who I had once served, and committed my life to. I was filled with anger and blamed God for all my failures.

I had gotten to a point in my own life so mad at God I could not hear him. At this point in 2013, I lived 5.5 hrs away from Immokalee. I had not listened to that unmistakable voice from the Lord for almost 20 years. I wanted nothing to do with Church or God.

I finally realized he had been with me all the time. It was my fault. I had left him. He was speaking; I just was not listening. He has always been walking with me every minute of every day. He never leaves us. We leave him. I finally woke up and realized that I was living a much better life than I could ever have in Immokalee.

> *Deu 31:6 Be strong and courageous. Do not be afraid or terrified because of them, for the LORD and your God goes with you. He will never leave you and not forsake you*

It was a Miracle how my Lord could love me so much that he would again want to use me after almost 30 years after building the facility on the PROMISED LAND in the 1980s. But, instead, he used me again, a sorry, no-good sinner, unfaithful sinner, who had been mad at him and blamed him for the terrible events that happened to me in my life's JOURNEY.

I will go into more detail about this situation later in this book. However, I consider it one of the many Miracles in this Long life's Journey to the Promised Land.

But at this point, so that the reader can follow along in the Journey, I believe it is important to mention my state of mind and location in 2013.

The reader needs to understand I had left Immokalee in 1994 ashamed of myself because of my business failures. I moved to Fl. Keys. I was once a wealthy and successful businessman. Blessed by my Lord in every business venture I started. In the 1980's I lived in a vast country home on 10 acres. The Lord had truly blessed me, starting from nothing.

These statements are written not to be a bragger but to give the reader insight into the author of this book. I was a person who had given his all to his Lord, teaching Sunday school for years, a deacon. I was a person who opened and shut the church's doors for many years. I was a person who witnessed too many others one on one for his Lord. Many people came to know my Lord because of a visitation program the Lord led me to develop. Over 125 souls were saved in one year because of this program. It was the main reason we needed to build a larger church facility.

I was a person who went with his family to every Sunday Morning, Sunday night, and Wednesday night service. I was a person who donated two years of his life to building the new Church facility, with 0 monetary rewards. I was a person who donated 1000s of dollars to the building fund and the church. I have never moved my membership from the Immokalee First Baptist Church, although I now regularly attend Church in the Florida Keys.

How could the Lord let my business ventures fail? I had given him my all. I closed all my business ventures on Sunday. One of my many business ventures was a small grocery store. Our best day of business was Sunday. Plus, I did not allow this store to sell Alcohol. My business Logo was "In God We Trust." How could my Lord let this kind of person fail in business and have to file bankruptcy in the 1990s?

I was MAD AS you can be with my Lord, and I stopped talking (praying) to him and had lost faith in him. I lost my confidence in my Lord. I gave up on him. Thank God he did not give up on me. It is true he is long-suffering and will never leave us.

About 20 years later, I woke up after blaming God for my failures and realized that what had happened to me was for good. I write about these in detail to give the reader an understanding of my mindset. So they can understand my Journey to the Promised Land. So that the reader may also examine their lives to determine if similar things have happened to them,

I bet many other Christians can relate to this story—that something their life made them turn from God. Satan uses many things to test our faith, and those of us weak in our faith fail the test of Job and leave our father in heaven. Hopefully, this story will also speak to the others who have lost the belief that God loves them and became mad at their God.

I finally just started thinking a little more positively 20 years later after moving to the FL Keys and began to realize. However, I had been through an unbelievably hard time, which I would never want to go through again. However, I was in the best place possible for me. I began to realize although I had lost all the material gifts, my Lord had provided me with a better life. A much harder life but a lot more fun life in becoming a Charter boat Captain and starting a new business from scratch, having very few assets. This business is still thriving today. Look it up on the net MainAttraction.org. I sold it to my son Marty in 2017.

I began to understand that although it was tough to start all over from scratch, I spent time on the Atlantic Ocean and saw things few people had seen. It had always been a dream life goal that I wanted much later in life. I have always loved to fish and have been fishing since I was a young boy. I spent time with my two sons and wife now, which I did not have time for when I was in business in Immokalee.

After about 20 years of being unfaithful and mad at my Lord, I finally began to understand that I was much happier in the Keys than I could have even been in Immokalee as a successful business person. I finally realized that I was much better off and more content than staying in Immokalee. I finally began to pray and talk with my Lord again. I began to develop a different attitude and thank him for the bad things that forced me to leave my home and church and start all over. I finally woke up from the long darkness in my life's journey. I was just beginning to renew my relationship with my Lord. Within a short time, another Miracle happens in my life.

What a waste of time. Twenty years I separated myself from my Lord. Yet, he was with me all the time. I pray that he will forgive me for doubting him. When you take time to analyze, there are no other options to a happy and content life than having a relationship with God. There was a natural awaking. I began talking and walking with God again. I could feel his presents in me again.

One evening late, I overheard my wife talking to her sister on the phone in March 2013. MIRACLE

She was a member of the First Baptist Church of Immokalee. I overheard her tell my wife that 23 members just voted to sell the Church Facility. The first question is how I heard the conversation since I was at least 20 feet away from the phone my wife was talking on? I believe I heard and understood every word said about the vote to sell the promised Land. It had to be the Lord letting me hear the conversation.

It is another one of the times the Lord spoke to me clearly and directly.

He said, "Morris, you have to go back to Immokalee and save my Church." As soon as my wife hung up the phone, I told her we had to go back to Immokalee. My wife was shocked since I had not gone back to Immokalee in 20 years. I would not even consider returning until this moment. It was a 5.5 hr. drive both ways.

As this book goes forward, you will read how the Lord used me to build his Church facility in the 1980s, how he used me to reach the Churches dream to reach the Promised Land. As you read this story, you will understand how God prepared me in my life's Journey for the task he wanted me to accomplish for him in the future.

God inspired me to write the original edition of this book which helped save the Promised Land from destruction. He later encouraged me to revise it in 2020. I used the original manuscript as a foundation to communicate truths that may help many others like me, who may have lost their way. But now, I believe he wanted me to publish this book so all can better understand how God works in all believers' lives as he guides them in the journey to their promised land.

I hope the reader can follow the back in forth of events from the past to the future. I also how the reader will understand the many side streets I travel down as my Lord puts these thoughts in my mind.

We are going back to 2013, then to the beginning 100 years ago, and then to the MIRACLES that happened on the Journey to the Promised Land. The Miracles are the foundation of this book. So please do not stop reading this book until you get to the Miracles. The Journey is long and will illustrate how God works and is always with you even in the bad times.

The decision to sell the Promised Land would have been the destruction of the Church in Immokalee. Hence, this event, although a wrong decision, inspired this book.

The fact is that voting to sell the Church facility even done with good intentions dishonors so many sacrifices. So many gave time and money to make the Church building possible, thinking as we all did at that time, and were even told, that this Church building was the will of God, and it would stand as a light for Immokalee forever until it is overflowing with saved souls.

Again, I hope this true story is not misunderstood by people who believe it builds up Morris Lewis's ego. This true story points out that I was unworthy, and I give my Lord the praise and all the credit. He did it all and used me in some small way, muddling through as he inspired my mind, spirit, thoughts and directed my path in my daily walk with him. I was only willing to let him use me.

I did nothing except listen to him and ask him to direct my path, thoughts, and spirit.

As I wrote this book, I already knew that Satan would use this story and tell some it is not true and that I would be humiliated by some. Some did in 2013, and others did it again in 2020. Some will not listen, and others will make fun of me for writing it. I am not a Prophet, that is for sure. The Bible says that a Prophet is not a Prophet in his town. Jesus was rejected in his hometown of Bethlehem. It almost always seems like those who know us the closes, our friends, are the ones who doubt our motives the most.

> *Mark 6:V. 4: But Jesus said unto them, A prophet is not without honor, but in his own country, and among this own Ken, and in his own house.*

Those who have ears, I pray they will hear.

In 2013 after I learned about the decision to sell Promised Land, the Lord directed me to visit the church. After attending a Church service, I felt compelled to write this book.

This book is not intended to hurt anyone, but I believe they are necessary to understand Immokalee's church history. There may be other churches that could be facing similar issues. This book may provide them with some insight into handling similar situations and challenges. It may also help individuals understand that most Church families have issues as any typical physical family would.

Some may say the book is more about the background than the actual Miracles in the building process. But I believe that the history, details, and past experiences had to be put into a definite order before the church could be built. This is **THE JOURNEY**. Most of the **MIRACLES** that you could see and touch happened during the building process of the facility in the 1980s. But also some Miracles happen, getting us to the place of starting the building process. These Miracles were just as important, maybe even more critical.

I have considered whether or not to include these side streets, as I called them, in this story and have come to the firm conclusion that they should be part of this book. Hoping that some reading these sections will be encouraged and their faith increased as they may look back at their own lives to determine, recall and recognize, that the Lord has been walking by their side all the time, for many years even though they may not have realized it.

If you wish to only read about the **MIRACLES** that happen in the Church building, you may want to skip forward to that part of this book. Although I believe the background and side streets, **THE JOURNEY** will help get a comprehensive understanding of how my Lord works in the daily lives of those that know and love him.

LET us BEGIN this long Life's JOURNEY TOGETHER: The Background and Foundation:

It is a very long story and started 107 years ago. I believe the Lord foresaw the future and wanted the church to be built at its present location, at the corner of Lake Trafford Road and Highway 27, the center of Immokalee, Florida. I researched the church's history and discovered the church was started in 1913. The history of the First Baptist Church of Immokalee can be found at WWW.fbcimmokalee.org. I am not sure who wrote this, or am I convinced that all these details are correct.

In 2020 there is an updated modern website will be available at https://www.fellowshipchurch.co/. It does not include the early history of the church. The website does include current events of what is happening on the PROMISED LAND today. I suggest that you do not go to it until after reading this book. If you do, you will not understand the suspense and journey this book is about. You will be reading the conclusion before understanding the Journey to the Promised Land.

I have contacted the past pastors and sent them unedited copies of the manuscripts to make comments and correct any errors in the texts or dates. Brother Babb Adams and Brother Larry Finely were very helpful and encouraged me to continue this book. Further, they encouraged me to get it published.

Now let us get back to the long JOURNEY TO THE PROMISED LAND:

Please always keep in mind the **JOURNEY**, the roads, paths, events that guided my life, and others to finish the task of getting to the **PROMISED LAND**, starting in 1913. The **Promised Land** completed the church facility in 1986, located at Highway 29 and Lake Trafford.

Although we had reached the PROMISED LAND in 1985, we continue on our JOURNEY, as all Christians continue on their Life's Journey. This book focuses on the history and details of the JOURNEY. It also details what happened in 2013 when some wished to abandon and sell the PROMISED LAND.

Since the church's foundation in Immokalee in 1913 was destined to reach Promised Land.

I believe that dedicated Godly men and women years before reaching the Promised Land were inspired by God to do the things they did. I also am one of those men, and I have written about how the Lord in my Life's Journey prepared me to do what I know was his will.

I heard that the Roberts Family donated the Property many years ago, the PROMISED LAND. Therefore, the following conclusions are based on what I was told.

The Donated funds used to purchase the "Promise Land," the new location of the First Baptist Church Immokalee, according to Brother Babb Adams pastor 1969-1981

After discovering the above history of the church online, I phoned Brother Babb Adams, who was pastor during the purchase and asked him to tell me what happened. He has permitted me to use his words. I have also mailed Brother Babb a copy of this book to ensure this history's details are correct.

Dice Roberts Church elder's leadership to the "Promised Land":

According to Brother Babb Adams, "the Roberts family, and Red Cattle Company, primarily under Dice Roberts leadership, donated the funds and set up a special account, in the church used to purchase the property Highway 27 and Lake Trafford Road". The second property, the back lots at the west end, was purchased from Bryon Royall. However, the funds to buy the property came from the particular account set up, and the funds were donated by Red Cattle Company or by Dice Roberts to purchase the present location for the church.

The "Promised Land" Best location in Immokalee:

Brother Babb believed that it was a MIRACLE, that the best location Immokalee was purchased for a future site for a new Church. He called it the Promised Land. The Roberts Family, especially Dice Roberts, let the Lord guide them to make this purchase. "<u>Brother Babb believed that this was God's plan. He also believed that the property should never be sold</u>." He believed that could not be replaced, that it is wrong, and dishonors those in the past who did so much to make the new building possible. He believed it was wrong to sell it, as was being considered by the church in 2013.

There will never be a Church built on the corner of Highway 29 and Lake Trafford Road (the Promised Land). A newspaper front-page article in the Immokalee Bulletin stated this when the land was purchased.

Brother Babb shared some history with me. One item was that when the church purchased the property, Stan, the editor of the Immokalee bulletin at that time, had a full front-page article about the purchase and stated that "a new Church would not ever be built on that land since it was too valuable." This property on the corner of Highway 29 and Lake Trafford Rd. has 1000 ft of highway frontage was on 29 and 800 ft of frontage on Lake Trafford road. It was in the center of the new Immokalee.

We know today that was not a correct statement. Our Lord had a different plan, and I believe my Lord directed our past church leader's path to start the process.

This picture is a picture of Highway 29 and the corner of Lake Trafford Road. It now has lots of businesses all around it. When the property was purchased, there were no businesses in the area.

Jack Queen donates dump trucks, and Collier Company donates the fill dirt to fill in a pound years before construction begins on the Promised Land, under Brother Babb's ministry.

Brother Babb told me another fantastic piece of history that happened in the early days of the 1970s concerning fill dirt. This event occurred a second time while we were in the process of building the church in 1985. It was almost an exact repeat of the event.

In the back of the property, on the Promised Land, there was a pound. I remember it. It was on the property in the north-east corner. Collier Company had dug a small lake and had piled fill dirt on the road's side, just on the other side of the Promised Land. It was just sitting there. Brother Babb thought this dirt would be just enough to fill up the pound on the Church property in the southwest corner. Remember, this happened years before the construction of the church.

Collier Company asked if the Church could use the dirt from their new sub-division. They said yes. Jack Queen was a church member in the heavy equipment business in the 1970s. He agreed to move the dirt for fuel costs only. Brother Babb said that Jack Queen never sent a bill to the church for the fuel. He also had an essential role in building the facility in 1985, written about later in this book. God Bless Jack Queen. He is a foundation cornerstone and building block of the church used in building the New Church facility in 1985.

It was nice to talk to Brother Babb again. He was much older. His mind was clear as a bell, especially about the subject we were discussing, THE JOURNEY TO THE PROMISED LAND. He remembered the details that are in this book. I do not believe the fact that we both could remember events so clearly was by accident. He was much older than I was, but we both had clear hindsight in the accrued events. I love and respect him and I will talk more about him, later in this book, in his role in getting to the Promised Land.

The Bible points out in many true stories in the old and New Testament that God had preplanned and, in his foreknowledge, set certain events into motion. These events were set into motion before I was born. I believe my Lord still does this today.

I am not familiar with the details or what inspired the Roberts Family/Dice Roberts to purchase the location and the insight to buy the best site in Immokalee for a new Church, even before Immokalee was a real town. Through my research from 1944-1948, O. O. Roberts was a pastor, but I do not believe he was related to the Roberts family, who founded the Red Cattle Company. Immokalee was only a cow town back then. However, as a young boy, I can remember Main Street as a dirt road, not paved and places to tie up horses, in front of a business. Others will have to add to this part of this story.

I hope to get more details of the history and add it to this true story. Maybe someone else will write this part of this story. I understand that the brief history of the church from the internet printed states that the church purchased the property. It gives some insight into the church from the beginning.

I believe that it is essential that the history of all churches be, written, saved, and updated so that future generations will understand how things happen. In addition, history could be helpful so that the new generations will not make the same mistakes as the past generation.

God Bless the Roberts family's elders for letting Lord use them and listen and obey his call, especially Dice Roberts.

Therefore I believe this may have been the first **MIRACLE** that the Roberts family let the Lord use for the foundation of the Church building, "The Promised Land." There were probably many more miracles, but I can't attest to them since I was not born yet or very young. However, without the "Promised Land" and location for the new church, the New Church building would not have been built. The property was in the center of the new Immokalee, which would come for many years in the future.

Not the old downtown Immokalee, where the church I grew up in was. At that time, the old church was also in the center of the old town Immokalee. There seems to be a trend here. In both cases, God wanted his church to be in the center of town. I believe this is where he wants to be in our hearts. God wants to be in the center and focal point of our lives. He also requires the first fruits of our lives.

How they foreknew the perfect and best location at that time was another miracle. There were no buildings in that area. I believe they had to have been led by God to select the perfect and best location for our Lord's Church. Undoubtedly, the spirit of our Lord directed them.

It is hard to list each action the Lord influenced since there were so many small steps in the process of reaching his goal. However, it would be wise to mark them in bold print. With hindsight, it is easy to understand they were all working together at the same time over many years.

God's foreknowledge and plan:

<u>I believe</u> that the **Lord** took all the many parts, events of life, and people he needed to build his church and put things and lesions in life to prepare them for the significant challenges he had foreseen. Many of those involved were not even aware that the Lord would use them in his overall plan to build his church.

The following few sections are about the Author, Morris Lewis, the background of my personal experiences, trials, and events that molded my life to prepare it for a considerable task God had for to do many in the future:

I know the experiences in my life's journey prepared me from a young boy. A boy who had been on his own since he was about 13 years old with no assets, no family to be disciplined by, directed by/led. Without me being aware that I was being prepared to do the task for the Lord in the future.

I only played a tiny part in the overall plan. Still, if any of those others did not follow the call and leadership of the Holy Spirit, I often wondered if the Church facility on the Promised Land would have even come to reality.

<u>I believe,</u> just like the Children of Abraham, those who are willing to be used, even if they were not aware of it, were being prepared for a massive task in the future. However, it stills amazes me how each of the many parts/events had

to take place in a definite order to make the new Church Building a reality.

There is a very similar pattern in the Old Testament writings about Abraham, David and how God influenced their paths to establish Israel's nation.

A very bright light appeared to me one night when I was a child:

I am a product of a broken home and fight every night between my mother and many step<u>fathers</u>. When I was about 11 years old, the fight was so bad that I climbed under the bed frightened. I was scared to death. I knew a little about Jesus and believed in him as a child.

> *Matt 18:V 1-7: V2 And Jesus called a little child unto him and set him in the midst of them. V 3: And said, Verily I say unto you, Except ye be converted, and become as little children, y shall not enter into the kingdom of heaven.*

I am not sure if I was asleep or awake; it was so many years ago. But I will never forget it. I saw a bright light, and someone/something, maybe an angel. I was not sure what appeared to me and but it said, "Fear not, you are going to be OK; I have great plans for you in the future." You are going to do something, with my help, extraordinary and unique for me. "I will be with you always." It could have been a **<u>MIRACLE</u>**.

Luke 2:10 and the <u>angel said</u> unto them, Fear not, for behold I bring you good tidings of great Joy, which shall be to all people.

My childhood background was without any parental guidance. My father died when I was ten years old. My mother and father had separated many years before. I just could not live with my mother. I was on my own by the time I was 13-14 years old. I mostly supported myself by working in various jobs starting from the 9th grade.

My Spiritual Birthday Certificate: Tent Revival Farmers Market 1960: (Aside street)

John 5:13: These things, have I written unto you that believe on, the name of the Son of God, <u>that ye may know</u> that ye have eternal life, and that ye may believe on the name of the Son of God.

I went to a tent revival on New Market Road, Immokalee, in 1960. I remember clearly what that Evangelist said, "You need to claim this date and remember it, as the day that you were saved. In the future, if Satan attempts to steal the joy of your salvation by telling you that you are not saved; you can confront Satan with that specific date. I have used this many times in my young Christian to fight off Satan's fiery dart attracts when I had sinned and started wondering if I was saved. Wondering if I was saved, how in the world could I have done this evil thing.

Romans 3:23 All have sinned and come short of the glory of God.

Therefore, I have always claimed Nov. 6, 1960, as the date that I was saved. I could have been saved earlier but was unsure since I was so young when I accepted Jesus as my Savior and the Lord of my life. I had used this date many times in my life when Satan tried to get me to doubt my salvation experience. Satan has said to me, Morris, you cannot be saved. A Christian would not do that evil deed. You must have lost your salvation. Satan used this deception to separate the believer from their Lord.

I do not believe that you can ever lose your salvation. It is a gift from God.

Romans 5: V. 18 Therefore, as by the offense of one judgment came upon all men to condemnation, even so by the righteousness of one the gift come upon all men unto justification of life.

God does not take back his promises and what he has given us. By Grace, we are saved, not by anything we can do ourselves.

: otherwise work is no more work Romans 11:V. Six and if by grace, then is it no more of works: otherwise grace is no more grace. But if it be of works, then is it no more grace.

We cannot lose it. It is forever. We may lose the joy of our salvation and also may be out of our Lord's will, but we are still saved. Our Lord uses different techniques to get our attention on earth. He sometimes has to chasten his children.

> *Hebrews 12:6: <u>For</u> <u>whom</u> the <u>Lord</u> <u>loveth</u> he <u>chasteneth</u>, <u>and</u> <u>scourgeth</u> <u>every son whom</u> he <u>receiveth</u>.*
>
> *7: <u>If</u> ye <u>endure</u> <u>chastening</u>, <u>God</u> <u>dealeth</u> with <u>you</u> <u>as</u> with <u>sons</u>: <u>for what son</u> is <u>he whom</u> the <u>father</u> <u>chasteneth not?</u>*
>
> *8: <u>But</u> <u>if</u> ye <u>be</u> <u>without</u> <u>chastisement</u>, <u>whereof all</u> <u>are</u> <u>partakers</u>, <u>then</u> are <u>ye</u> <u>bastards</u>, <u>and</u> <u>not</u> <u>sons</u>.*

If we do not experience our Lord's chastening, we should examine ourselves to make sure we are saved.

> *Matt 7:23: And then will I profess unto them I never knew you depart from me ye that work iniquity.*

Went these doubts come, I would fire back at him, in my mind, the date of my <u>Spiritual Birthday, Nov 6, 1960</u>, and he would flee from me and leave me alone.

> *James 4: V. 7. Submit yourselves, therefore, to God, Resist the devil, and he will flee from you.*

I would strongly suggest that everyone remember their spiritual birthday. The exact date is not a significant issue; if you do not retain, choose a date you believe is the closest date. We remember our natural birth date. How much more important is it to reflect our Spiritual birth date.

When people are saved in their church, I have often wondered why churches do not print out a Spiritual Birth Certificate.

A person only has to come as a child, recognize they are a sinner, ask for forgiveness, believe, and my Lord will save them.

Romans 10:13: For whosoever shall call upon the name of the Lord shall be saved

I believe that Satan steals the joy of many who have had a salvation experience. If a person can remember their human birth date, it is even more critical to retain their spiritual birthday. If they were issued a spiritual birthday certificate, it would be a great tool to fight off the fiery darts of doubt that Satan, when we doubt our salvation.

When Satan tempted me in this area to doubt my salvation, I said to Satan, "depart from me, "on Nov. 6, 1960, was my spiritual birthday". On that day, my name was written into the Lambs Book of Life.

Revelation 20:11-15: And whosoever was not found written in the book of life was cast into the lake of fire.

Bessie Taylor Christian women and saint of God: You never know whose life your witness will influence.

In a few years, I believe I was on my own, 13-14 years old. I stayed with Bessie Taylor, a saint that walked to Church every Sunday. If someone did not pick her up, she would shuffle to the Church Sundays day and night and Wednesday night for prayer service, even with her bad knees. I do not believe I ever really appreciated her pain until I needed a new hip, and my wife had to have back and knee surgery.

You could see that she was in pain, but she still walked, and I do not remember her complaining. She was faithful to her Lord. The church was about 4 miles or more from her home. I believe that she never asked anyone to pick her up and drive her to the church, although many people did. Brother Babb could attest to her witness more than me. Her witness had a significant bearing on my life. She was soft-spoken and rarely said anything. She was penniless. But her actions as a real Christian spoke loudly to all who came in contact with her.

> *Mark 12: V 42-44: And he called unto him his disciples, and saith unto them. Verily I say unto you, This poor widow hath cast more I than all they who have cast into the treasury: V44 For all they did cast in of their abundance, but she cast in all that she had even all her living.*

She had few material things. You could have said even on that day, and she lived in a shack. But you can believe that she now lives in a large mansion in heaven. Her faith was her witness. Her actions in her faith had a significant influence on my life. I wonder if you have ever known such a person in your life. Her efforts proved her faith. Because of her witness to me, I became a much better person and a stronger believer in Christ.

Big Skipper, You never know who is watching you: (Side Street)

Jumping many years in the future, 1995-2015, I was a very successful charter boat Capt. I do not know why the Lord laid this on my heart to share in this book.

In the last few years, a captain friend called "Big Skipper" was dying in the hospital. I believe he drank too much alcohol and was overweight, and had heart issues. I liked him, and he was full of fun, and he could tell the best stories. I phoned him one night while he was on his death bed, and we talked about the Lord. He told me he was saved and ready to go. He shared with me something that I was not aware of.

The Charter business is seasonal. I know that it is against God's commandments to work on Sundays. However, I believed it was necessary to work in my business due to my lack of faith. Therefore, I shut down all my business ventures on Sundays when I lived in Immokalee. God honored and continued to bless those businesses for many years without them being open on Sunday. But one thing I did continue to practice was shutting my boats down on Christmas and Easter. To my knowledge, no one else in Marathon in the charter business did this.

Big Skipper said that night on his death bed, "Morris, you know what I respected about you most, "You always shut your business down Christmas and Easter." That was a witness to me, he said. I had no idea that he felt that way or even noticed. Now I am wondering how much a greater witness I could have been if I had the faith and courage to shut down my charter business on Sunday, also. I am trying to make that you never know who is watching and how much influence you have on someone else's life. But, as the Bible teaches, I still believe that it is wrong to work on Sunday, even your manservants.

> *Exodus 20:3-17. V. 8 and 9 Remember the Sabbath day, to keep it holy. V: 9: Six days shalt thou labor and do all thy work.*

I pray that I will get back the faith I once had and be able to shut down my charter fleet on Sundays. But it is a callous decision to make, especially under the world's current economic conditions. But, of course, and my wife and I go to church every chance we get. Many of our customers say that fishing is not working. I am joking here, but I wonder if my Lord would also think that way. But to me, it is a lot of enjoyable hard work, 24-7.

Another person life is changed, and I was not aware of my witness to him: {another side street}

Another story was when a captain I had hired to run a boat I found out later had a drug issue. I later learned this, and he had many other matters. He came by the dock ten years later and said he was now a Christian. He said his life was changed, and now it had a purpose. I believe as he told me that my Christian life's witness to him helped him change his whole life years later. So again, you never know who is watching your witness. I pray that my Lord will renew my spirit and give me that kind of faith so that my daily walk will be a witness for him, and he will give me control over my tongue and many other issues in my life.

Most of the people who influenced my life have passed and gone to be with my LORD.

2 Co 5:8: We are confident I say and willing rather be absent from the body and to be present with the Lord.

There are also more people who I write about later in this book that influenced my life. One of the facts that I hold upon in my heart is that I will see them again one day in heaven. The book by Norman Vincent Peale, The Power of Positive Thinking, had a powerful impact on my life at a young age and continues through today. In chapter 16, he writes about his belief in the afterlife.

This one statement of many which had stayed with me: "For my part, when I gained the unshakeable belief that there is no death, that all life is indivisible, that the here and hereafter are one, that time and eternity are inseparable, that he is one unobstructed universe, then I found the most satisfying and convincing philosophy of my entire life."

He writes about many examples of those on their death beds who see just before passing their friends and others welcoming them to a beautiful place. IT IS A MUST READ for those who have a fear of death.

One day, I took out a lady on my Charter boat that had a weak heart. She was revied back to life five times. She had 5 of her very close friends with her on my boat at that time. All verified that her story of the five times she was brought back to life from death was a fact. I believed her. She was so sincere. She spoke about seeing her father and others who had passed and in heaven, seeing her friends that it was a beautiful place, and she did not want to return. I told her that she should write a book about her experiences. It was compelling.

None of us want to die. There is a natural fear about it. I believe God has put it there; otherwise, we would all kill ourselves to go ahead and go to heaven.

I believe at the time of death, the Christian believer will get peace at the time death passes all understanding and will be confident that our Lord will do what he has promised.

> *2 Co 5:8: We are confident I say and willing to be absent from the body and to be present with the Lord*

> *Phil 1:6: Being confident of this very thing that he which hath begun a good work in you will perform it until the day of Jesus Christ*

Again let me encourage you to read this powerful book, "The Power of Positive Thinking by Norman Vincent Peale. It is only 9.95 on Amazon.

I give my Lord and Savior all the Glory and Praise:

My intent here is not to provide myself with any praise but to give my Lord all the credit for what he did in my life. After thinking of my experience, I have grown to understand how my Lord has been there, walking with me and directing my path for my entire life.

But I believe this is a book that the Lord wanted me to write, and maybe, that is why he had kept me alive—especially considering even when, sometimes in the past, I had requested to be taken home to heaven. I do believe his spirit is helping me write this true story. Not for my benefit only, but for others to understand my Lord's miracles while building the First Baptist Church in 1985-86. I can feel his mighty spirit and directing almost every word I put on paper. Not the missed spelled words or poor grammar, but the content and intent of those words. I pray that my flesh will be controlled and that my spirit will still and listen to what the Lord wants me to write. Some parts of this true story could be hurtful, but this is not the intent of this book. My Lord loves everyone, especially sinners and the sheep that have gone astray. I consider myself one of the worse sinners and do not deserve how my Lord has blessed me. Or how he watched over me and took a particular interest in me.

Luke 15: V 3-V7: I say unto you that likewise, joy shall be in heaven over one sinner that repenteth, more than over ninety and nine righteous persons, who need no repentance.

My Lord's intent, the loving Shepard, is not to condemn but to tell all that he loves them and has compassion for them. He wants the best for them in life on earth and in heaven. All his laws and commandments so that if we followed and obeyed them, we would have a better life, an abundant life, and a happy, fulfilled life.

John 10: V. 10-11: The thief cometh not but to steal, and to kill, and to destroy; I have come that they might have life and that they might have it more abundantly. .V.11: I am the good shepherd; the good shepherd giveth his life for his sheep.

A life that is not free from trials, sorrows, and heartbreaks. But a life trusting our Lord for everything. We must understand that all things work together for good for those who love him.

Romans 8:28. We know that all things work together for good to them that love God, to those who are called according to his purpose.

All that my Lords ask are two simple rules for us to live by:

Remember what Jesus said; all we needed to do was obey only two simple common sense principles. Love the Lord with all your mind, heart, and soul, and love your neighbor as yourself.

> *Luke 10:27 "Thou shalt love the Lord thy God with all thy heart, and with all thy soul, and with all thy strength, and with all thy mind, and love thy neighbor as thyself.*

Without this kind of Love, it is impossible to please God. If love is in your heart, you will not and cannot condemn others. Boy, this is the kind of love that is easy to talk about but very hard to practice.

Remember, "You cannot legislate righteousness." It was one of Brother Babb Adam's favorite statements of truth in life's journey, inspired by his Bible knowledge and through experiences in life that he has faced.

My Lord sends me to college to prepare for his future work for me:

I stayed/lived with Bessie in my high school days for a few years and then went off to college. It was a **Miracle** in my own life that I even had the opportunity to go to college. I only stayed in High School to play basketball. I loved playing it. Another story I hope to write. Later in life, I became the head basketball coach in Immokalee. My teachers, except for a very few, were terrible. They did not care nor motivate their students. However, I can remember a few good ones, Havel Chandler, Bud Tompkins, and Wayne Pringle. I do not believe it was by chance that they were all Christians, and later in my life, we became close friends when I became an adult.

I did not realize then how much influence they had on my life. You never know who is watching you. Your actions are your best witness.

I know that Satan is putting doubt in some of those in the Church of Immokalee reading this story; the person who is writing cannot be doing God's will. {Side Street}

Ephesians 2:V. 8-9: for by grace are ye saved. V9: Not of works, lest any man should boast.

As I have stated from the beginning, I am just a man. I am a sinner only saved by the grace of God. I have learned from God's word that none are perfect. If you wait until you are perfect, you will never get anything done for our Lord. That there will always be those against you, no matter how good your witness is. It is best not to even think about what others think about and do what you believe is God's will in your life. But do something. Put feet into your Prayer, as the old saying goes.

Put feet into your Prayers:

His pastor told an old story of a man who wished to remove a bar from the county. Later that night, a Miracle happened, and that place burned down. The pastor mentioned to the man about the Miracle of the burning down of the building. The man responded; you have to put "Feet into your Prayers." Just as the book for James says, faith without works is dead being alone. Of course, this is just an illustration, but it does get across the point; just wishing and only praying does not get the task done.

> *James 1:V8- But be ye doers of the word and not hearers only, deceiving your selves.*

> *James 2:20: But with thou know, O vain man, that faith without works is dead?*

I was the most unlikely and unusable person who is terrible in grammar and spelling was chosen to pen this book; God gets all the Glory:

In high school, I did not study. Mr. Havel Chandler was my 6th-grade teacher and my English teacher throughout high school. It was not his fault, but I never learned to spell and have always been terrible in grammar. Later in life, we would be friends and Christian brothers in our Church. Havel Chandler was a fine man and played the Organ in the old and new church building for years. He is the one who selected the organ and piano for the new church building.

I have always believed that Mosses and David were odd choices for the Lord to choose in the Old Testament. One Pharaoh's right-hand man, and the other only a Shepherd. It is strange because I have always been able to write words/thoughts, although my grammar and spelling have always been terrible.

My mind works so fast when writing; when I read the exact words, I read the correct phrases onto that page. I still see them as if they are on the page as I proofread them. My wife Linda had to type and proofread all my written assignments while I was in College my last two years. She should have gotten my diploma, not me.

I mention this because it is a miracle that the Lord would ask me or choose me to write this true story since; I am so terrible, not bad, but terrible in using English and cannot spell a word. Maybe, I just got the answer to why it has taken me so long to write this true story. We used the old bell typewriter in my days in school and college. You typed It sounded like a bell when you went to the following line, pick, pick, and then ding.

In the last few years, the charter business in the Keys has forced me to learn a little about the computer. I believe the computer may be the Beast in the Last Days with the mark of 666, but that is another complete and different story. Perhaps the Lord developed spell and grammar checks, just for me. However, the spelling is so far off and the grammar so poor that even my computer cannot figure it out.

Or the reason is that my Lord likes to use the most unusable and most unlikely person to do his work so that he will get all the Glory. He does this many times in the Bible as an example to let others know that it is the Lord doing the talking or working and not that person. Because they are so inadequate, with lack of the skills, in doing the task that others would recognize that it could only be the Lord working through that person. **IS THIS YOU?** I have found out that you only have to want to be used and have a willing heart, like David/Mosses/others, and our <u>Heavenly Father will provide everything needed</u>.

I should not have been able to go to college:

When I went to college, I had to start in the remedial program. I could not even do high school work, must less college work. But the College teachers challenged me, and after the first semester, I was ready for college classes and became an A student in most of the lessons I took for the next four years.

I did not have to take another English Class to get my diploma, but I indeed should have. But if I did, I probably would still be in college today. The point here is I should not have made it to college; all the odds were against me. I had to work in the day and go to school at night for my first two years to make money to live on and pay college fees. Remember, I had been on my own, with no parents to help since I was about 14 years old. I did not have any funds saved to pay for college expenses, yet somehow, I worked and earned the funds to put myself through college with my high school sweetheart's help.

The Lord sent a perfect helpmate and most beautiful woman in the whole world to me: Miracle

I called her Doll because her father did, but her name is Linda. But she is and always has been a Doll, to me. It is another **MIRACLE** in my personal life. Without her, I could have done nothing, and I would have been nothing. I believe the Lord bonded me with a perfect mate, whom I did not even want when I first met her.

I was madly in love with someone else from grade school to entering Jr. College. Of course, I had no idea what love was in those early days. But I thought that I could not live without this person. Remember the tent revival on New Market Road in 1960, where I learned to claim my spiritual birthday.

This is another excellent thing that happened to me at that revival. The evangelist made a statement that stayed with me. I wouldn't say I liked it at that time, but I have learned that it was authentic. You see, I only wanted this particular girl as my future mate. I did not care what the Lord wanted for me. I believed at that time, and I knew what was best. I always said, "Lord, have your will, but give me this." I always thought that I knew best. I finally understood that only God knows what is complete, perfect, and best for our lives.

God only gives perfect Gifts and knows what is best to provide us with so we can have an abundant life:

The Evangelist said to pray, **"Lord have your will, and it will be the best for you/me to have a perfect and abundant life."**

It is a different attitude and way of looking at life. God knows best and wants to give you good things. I did not like this statement, but it did stick with me until this day. I wish I had the faith to practice it more because, from hindsight, I have found out that most if not all the things that happen to me were for my best in the future, even though they were sometimes terrible to deal with in the present. All things work together for good,

> Romans 8:28. We know that all things work together for good to them that love God, to them who are called according to his purpose.

I should have had a stronger faith in many areas of my life. You would think that I would have learned my lesson by now, but I still try to have my will and not the Lord's will, path, which is always best. He only wants to give us the best. I just wonder how many abundant life opportunities I have missed in life's journey because I did not honestly seek God's will and relied upon my own will and understanding.

The first time I met my wife:

We are going to move forward. I am now in my first semester of college. I had just graduated from high school in June, and now it is Oct. This little girl with a lengthy pigtail came up to me at a Halloween dance in the Gym. in the old Immokalee High School. She asked me to dance. Whatever gave her the idea to ask me is beyond me. She was only in the 9th grade; I am now just entering college; I am now the big College man. I said no. I could not fast dance a lick at that time and still cannot even today since I do not have any rhythm. I could slow dance a little, but my wife taught me how to do that while dating. We now love to slow dance together.

> *Romans 14:14: I know, and am persuaded by the Lord Jesus, that nothing unclean of itself; but to him that esteemeth anything to be unclean, to him it is unclean.*

I now have left that dance, and time moves forward. I later see my future wife in the old Kent Theater in Immokalee. It was not too good even in those days, but it was a place to go. She was sitting with a classmate of mine whom I did not like. I do not know why, but I disliked him. He left his seat and went somewhere, maybe to get her something to eat, and I saw my opportunity to get to this classmate. So I made my move and sat beside her while he was gone.

She did not run me out of the seat. So I believed I was home free, and my classmate never returned to get his chair. I think Dr. No, a James Bond movie, was playing. Not sure how long I stayed in the seat, but the classmate I disliked never returned. Now I saw that twinkle in my future wife's eye, and I realized this was a time for a kiss. So we kissed bombs when off, bang, bang, boom, boom, fireworks, sparklers, and everything else for the first time. I fell madly in love with her that night.

I always told her that I wanted her young to train her just like I wanted since she was only in the 9th grade, but she coached and tamed me down. In those early days, I was a wild man. I was saved but still a very boisterous young man. We went steady for four years until she graduated from High School and married on June 21st, 1968. I hope that is the correct date. She will kill me if it is not. Just kidding, we are now happily married 53 years, and I am counting on another 50 years with this remarkable woman, My Doll.

Lord not my will but thy will: The abundant life:

This is another one of those side streets, but it is essential. I learned very young that you will have the very best if you listen to God. Not just a good thing, but a lasting thing, and perfect thing, my wonderful wife DOLL. This is what the Evangelist was staying in 1960 at the tent revival. Now I finally understand what he meant. We have been together for over 56 years in dating and marriage, and my love for her is stronger today than it was then. So, yes, we have had some excellent roads of life and some evil, but one thing we have always had was each other.

I consider her the best gift that my Lord ever has given me. One day I plan to write a book about our life together. This is a great love story that everyone should have the privilege to experience. But the purpose here is to point out again how the Lord was working in my life to give me the perfect mate, a helper to provide me with confidence, support, time, encouragement, and courage to do the work that the Lord had for me to do in the future.

I thank God almost every day for my wife, Doll (Linda Lewis). By the way, Linda, in Spanish, means beautiful. Guess what, my wife is Beautiful even today at the age of _____ cannot tell that, but she also has now and always has had a beautiful spirit.

More importantly, she has a beautiful Christian spirit and personality. We are a team as God has intended in his holy word. She makes decisions with emotions, and I decide with facts. Both are important in life. She believes in God's word and lets me be the head of the household. Still, I seek her advice on all critical decisions because we are not complete unless her emotions and my facts are needed to make crucial decisions.

Why she picked me a 110lb undernourished, small boy, 1st-year college is another Miracle. She sure put some weight on my bones with her great Southern cooking. Her mother taught her well. What she saw in me is the incredible miracle of the miracles. I renamed my wife, Sara, Abraham's wife's name. The Kings of the Old Testament still desired her in her old age. My wife is still beautiful in appearance and spirit. Again, I thank God daily in my heart for him putting us together. She has given me abundant life. By the way, I did not know it at the time, but my future wife also attended the same Revival in 1960. So was it by chance or by God's plan.

Moving on to the JOURNEY: The Lorded uses our Christian life experiences to prepare us for the future. (as seen by hindsight)

I still do not know how I made it. <u>I believe</u> from hindsight that the Lord had to have a hand in me getting into college, majoring in business and education, and graduating. I have known some just because they believe they are better than others because they have a college education. But I know many very successful millionaires and billionaires who do not have a college education. If you do not have a college education, do not worry about it. It is more important to have Jesus, and he will provide for you.

My intent is not to get sidetracked nor build myself up. On the contrary, I have always given my Lord praise and credit for the way he used me. But to continue to provide the reader with the understanding that I can see a few of the many steps in my own life, which the Lord used to prepare me for the future work he had planned for me. Maybe others will look back after reading this true story and meditate and think about how the Lord prepared them for life even through trials and other events in their life.

If I or any others had not let the Lord use them and prepared them for the tasks in his overall plan, I also believe that the Church building and or the Promise Land may not have happened. For example, if the Roberts had not let the Lord lead them to donate the funds to the church and set up a special fund to purchase the property and location in Immokalee. The Church located in the center of Old Immokalee's town would not have considered building a new Church Facility on Highway 27 in Immokalee and the corner of Lake Trafford.

Morris Lewis and many others involved in this JOURNEY to the Promised Land have been Church members for many years. I went to Sunday School there from grade school to 1995. The first pastor I remember was Brother L. E. Daniel. He was pastor from 1960-1963.

The youth programs had a tremendous and positive effect on my life then and in the future. I remember women of the Church like Mrs.

Later, Black, Mrs. Starling, and Jean Whisant witnessed to the youth through their leadership in the youth programs. All churches should have an expanding youth program. It takes special people to be involved with the youth program. Many may never know how their witness blessed and influenced the youth in these programs.

> *Proverbs 22: V6: Train up a child in the way he should go, and when he is old, he will not depart from it.*

God bless those who believe they have this particular calling, and they should be supported and respected by the Flock, the Church body. Steve Price, Bennie Zipperer, Karen, Kenny Hayden, Wayne, and Billie Chenny were a few standing against selling the Promised Land in 2013.

We designed the "Promised Land" Church building with our youth in mind. We built a Family Life Center to reach the youth for Christ and had family dinners together and many other related church functions. All Churches should focus on their youth. Without them, the Church will wither and die. We also designed and built a separate classroom for the different ages and a nursery for the very young.

But let's move on to the future of actual events, as I witnessed them and have a better understanding now looking back.

Brother Babb Adams and the Old Church Building in old town Immokalee: 1969-1981

Brother Babb Adams was the pastor. I love him to this day, and he helped me a lot in my personal and Christian life. I still think of him often. His wise two phrases he repeated continually, "You can't legislate righteousness" :>" Practice the presence of the Lord." He is the one who asked me to teach Sunday School, which forced me to study the Bible in a much different manner; getting prepared to teach is more demanding and forced me to learn. It is much easier to listen like a student. Being feed is more effortless than gathering the food/meat of the word.

> *James 3: V.1: My brethren, be not many teachers, knowing that we shall receive the greater judgment.*

Brother Babb is the one who, when I was struggling with a big decision of whether to continue to teach at Immokalee High School, helped me make the right decision from hindsight to leave that position which I loved and go into the business world. I have to believe this was all in God's plan for my life based upon hindsight and the events that took place later. I became a building contractor and hardware store owner.

The Church was not growing in the latter days of Brother Babb Adam's ministry in Immokalee. Brother Babb had been the pastor for many years. I do not remember all the details, but a few other members and I believed it was time to change leadership in the Church. None of us wished to harm Brother

Babb. We all loved him. He is and was a great man of God. The hardest thing I have ever had to do with two others was to approach him and suggest that he be better off and move to a different Church. The Church in Immokalee might start growing again if it had other leadership.

Brother Babb has done many good things in Immokalee, reached many souls, and grew his church for many years. But the Church was in decline. It was becoming cold, not increasing. Many members were leaving the church. The Church was in turmoil due to many different issues.

I understand that you are not to touch one of the Lord's anointed. All of those involved in this decision prayed and prayed for leadership from our Lord. We concluded that our church needed a different direction and supervision. In this case, with Brother Babb, our church was not growing. Sometimes it is suitable for the church members, men and women of God, in God's will, to take a stand and request that a pastor leaves the pulpit. <u>I only included this part in this book to give insight to the Church members in 2013 who dealt with unique issues.</u> Their problems were much different and <u>more severe</u> than those we had to deal with. But I have firmly come to this conclusion based upon hindsight based upon the many miracles and things that happened after Brother Babb's departure, which was good for him and the church. It was in our Lord's will, and it is alright to question the leadership. Brother Babb also agreed with this statement.

After talking with Brother Babb by phone in the last few days in May 2013, we both believe it was in our Lord's will. Under his leadership, he has done great work for our Lord after leaving the Church in Immokalee, building up two different Churches in Inverness, Florida. If a few men had not brought attention to the issues at that time, Brother Babb would probably not have left the Church in Immokalee until his death.

Another fantastic thing to me he did not remember me and the others who met with him and told him we believed it was time for him to vacate the pulpit at the First Baptist Church of Immokalee. I am not sure if he was kind to me, but I must take him at his word, for I know he is not a liar. I will remember that day forever, wondering until May 27, 2013, if we had done the right thing. Although I know we did the Lord's will, it is still a severe event when you touch the Lord's anointed. But it does point out that sometimes you have to take a stand, and it is in the Lord's will to do so, even with the leadership or pastor of your Church. But you had better be careful if you decide to take a stand and make real sure the Lord gives you direction and not your own will and emotions.

Throughout his Holly word in the Old Testament, the Bible teaches us to never divide the flock against one another. Brother Babb never did this, always showed concern for all his sheep, and still showed respect and love. I believe my experience with Brother Babb Adams, although a completely different situation, gave me an extraordinary insight into how to help the church of 2013 make some very tuff decisions.

James: 1: V.26 If any man among you seem to be religious, and bridleth not his tongue, but deceiveth his own heart, this man's religion is vain.

James 3: V.10. Out of the same mouth proceed blessing and cursing, My brethren these things ought not to so be.

When details are confused, issues are misled, and statements are disputed in later reports within weeks, division and confusion will cause conflict in that Church. Members will leave the Church rather than listen to that pastor. The Church will die from a lack of support from the actual Church members who have given up. Only a very few dare to take a stand and try to get others to see the truth. If the Church is not growing and reaching others for Christ, it hasn't any reason to exist. It would be better as a social club than a Church.

If that Church does not reach the youth, train and teach them, who will be the next generation? That Church is dead already; it just does not understand it yet. If you do not see any young people in the Church, there is something wrong with that Church's Leadership. Suppose you live in a community that has young people. The Bible again says:

Proverbs 22: V6: Train up a child in the way he should go, and when he is old, he will not depart from it.

The Shepherd has to lead for the Sheep to follow. He needs to be out in front of his flock, not following behind it. You cannot just blame the lack of growth of the Church on only the Sheep. The Shepherd is also responsible. Some pastors blame the Sheep, but they should be listening to their message and not be pointing their fingers at their sheep. I pray that those who have ears will hear. Since he departed from the First Baptist Church, I have seen Brother Babb Adams only once over the last several years. We are still friends and still love each other, and I respect him for his continued service for our Lord and the good fight he has continued for a lifetime. I know he will be rewarded when he reaches his final home in Heaven. Jesus will be there to welcome him, "Well Done, Thou Good and Faithful Servant."

Brother Babb decides to move to a different Church. But he never had ill will towards any of these brothers or sisters in Christ. Some believed his ministry was finished; others did not. So there were many hurt feelings and also confusion in the Church body. Yes, it was a trying time for the Church, but Brother Babb never took revenge on those who voted against him.

The future proves if our decision was the right decision and of God or our flesh. I believe that the decision was the right one and in God's Holy will from what happens in the future.

Brother Babb, I am sure at that time, was hurt; anyone would be, I believe, that he understands from hindsight that it was in God's overall plan that he leave at that time.

He had a considerable role in the building of the new Church. He paved the way for others to follow the foundation he had built. He set up a new building fund through his leadership, a percentage of the income. I am sure there were many other building blocks he laid in for the foundation to build a new Church Body and building.

Brother Babb Adams was the perfect fit when he was at the First Baptist Church. He had a cowboy-type personality, which blended in perfectly with the cowboy town of Immokalee at that time in history. But many believed his ministry was completed. Brother Babb had completed his mission.

<u>When we talked about the vote to sell the Promised Land, he told me that he believes it was a blessed holly property and should never be sold. He said that Satan had to have been part of this decision.</u>

During Brother Babb's vote of confidence, he wanted all the rules of the Church constitution to be followed. The Church By-laws required a Church vote. The Church body voted for a vote of confidence in the pastor. A special meeting was called. It was announced several Sundays before the vote was taken. All members were contacted, those in church regularly, and those not in church regularly. There was a secret ballot vote. Every detail was followed as per the Church by-laws. Yes, it was emotional. Yes, there was confusion. Everyone loved him. He had been a leader, friend, pastor, and preacher for us all for many years. Brother Babb did contact past members to support him. with their vote who had not been in the Church for many years.

There was a lot of politicking on both sides of the issue. **He won the vote to stay but quickly resigned in his wisdom and love for his Flock.** He loved his Church, his flock, and the members of that Church. He did not want to see the division in the Church. He tried to put the divided Church back together when he announced to the church that he believed it was time for him to move on. He was the excellent Sheppard who would give his life for his sheep.

He had finished the good fight. He said he had to take care of some crucial before the next pastor was appointed and continue the Lord's will for our Church. Only Brother Babb could have handled these particular issues, which hindered the future Church of Immokalee.

The main thing I remember was it was the most challenging moment of my life as a leader in the Church. I had to tell a man I loved that I believed his calling and time at First Baptist was over. Until recently, I wondered if I would have to give an account at the judgment seat for my role. Now I am more confident than ever that the two others and I did the right thing. It was very hard. We truly loved Brother Babb. We did not want to hurt him, but we believed it was time for a First Baptist change. I only write about this so that others who may be going through the same church issues may have courage. Only If they genuinely believe God's will that a pastor's work was finished. But you had better make sure; it is of God and not your flesh taking control of your mind and heart.

The decision concerning leadership in the church should be based upon Biblical facts and not feelings. When it is necessary to look at the facts, take a stand, and not just assume that 40% of the flock of a church is mistaken. If one or two of the sheep are not happy with the Shepherd is one thing, but if 40% of the flock has concerns, there must be something else wrong. A divided flock will not be an effective witness for the other sheep in the pastures or the loss. They are always watching those in the church. It gives Satan plenty of ammo to use.

If a few of the flock leaves the congregation due to what has happened in the Church, that is one thing. But when many the herd is looking for greener pastures, the deacons should be alarmed and search out facts, not emotions.

Those who do not have real factual knowledge should not blindly support a pastor or Church. They need to be informed and regularly attend business meetings. This, of course, goes both ways, those that support and those who do not help. Each should gather the facts and only look at the facts, not with emotions, but with reason, compassion, and love. Our Lord has taught us to do so.

I felt terrific after talking with Brother Babb for a brief moment or two at Home Coming service a few years back after he preached a fine sermon in Immokalee. He was older, and I was wiser. He has always been very wise. He was the same great man of God that I had always loved and thought that he was.

I phoned Brother Babb on May 15, 2013, and again on May 27, 2013, and he told me how the Lord had used him to lead his new Church in Inverness, Florida, to purchase a 50-acre plot. He said there were between 500 and 1000 people in his new Church. He had been preaching three services. Later, he was used to developing and pastoring another Church. He led the way to purchase a 23-acre plot with the Lord's direction and help him develop other new Churches. After learning this today, I must confirm that the actions a few of us took, was in the Lord's will. If we had not taken those actions, there might not have been a new Church Building in Immokalee. Nor would Brother Babb build those others in which Brother Babb was involved later. <u>This brings me to my point and why I have included the section in this book</u>. <u>What if the Promised Land was not sold? How many more souls could be saved in the future?</u>

I often had thought in my simple selfish mind, not under-standing the wisdom of God that Brother Babb leaving paved the way for the building of three new Church facilities. But with God, even a more remarkable event took place that until recent days just learned about the other facts that God had used Brother Babb to build two additional churches reaching 1000s for our Lord. Therefore, this was even a greater Miracle than I once thought.

I believe I am finally at peace with myself on this issue of being one of the three men who suggested that it was time for Brother Babb to relocate.

I believe the Lord has been preparing me for many years using life experiences and giving skills needed to build his New Church Building:

Many years before I even knew about the Promised Land and the preparation of others for the new Church building,

I believe after reflecting that the Lord had his hand in preparing me for the construction of the Church Building. It is one of the many reasons I believe the Church building is critical and should remain in its present location until our Lord comes back.

To get a complete understanding of the future events and the many **MIRACLES** coming in the church's actual building, I can only write about what I have seen and was a part of. I am sure there are others who God directed and made events happen that led their paths to prepare them for their future work, although at that time, they nor I had any idea what he was doing. I invite them to contact me and share their story with me.

> *Romans 8:28: And we know that all things work together for good to them that love God, to them who are the called according to his purpose."*

All things work for good for those who are called to his purpose. I believe this has further-reaching over the period than I once thought. I have read this verse for 30 years or more but have just recently understood it in a different context, that sometimes, it may take years for good to be recognized. I want everything done in a moment. But God looks at the long term and always makes the best decision. It is hard for our minds to comprehend with God; time is forever.

> *2 Peter 3: V. 8: But, beloved, be not ignorant of this one thing, that one day is with the Lord as a thousand years, and a thousand years as one day.*

More important bad events in our lives the Lord can turn them out for good in the future, although they were very stressed when we went through those bad events.

I do not know about you, but I am not good at waiting on the Lord to act. I want it done in my time, but my Lord sees and understands the total picture, and his timing is perfect. My timing could be hurtful or even harmful to God's overall plan. This point is driven home throughout the Old Testament stories of the prophets and the Children of Israel.

The Children of Israel kept doubting the Lord, and going their way, without having faith in God's timing, murmured against him and his perfect plan for them.

Many times the things that were happening to us at that time were not good at all, even destructive, stressful, and may not have been in God's will, but they still happened. It is a shame, but God does not always have his will followed. If it were, everyone would be saved.

> *John 3:16* *"For God so loved the world, that he gave his only begotten Son, that whosoever believeth in him should not perish, but have everlasting life."*

It is his will that all are saved, but in reality, few are. It is the Lord's will that none should perish. God does not send us to Hell. We send ourselves to Hell. It is our free will that God allows us to use to make decisions and choices.

Romans 7:18 "For I know that in me that is, in my flesh dwelleth no good thing: for to will is present with me, but how to perform that which is good I find not."

In my own life, I can think of many times when I doubted my Lord's plan and had to suffer the stress in life because I did not have enough faith to trust my father. I will use the experiences in my own life to point out this fact in this book. I believe the Lord prepared me all my life for the future, using both good and bad events to mold me to be useable for him. I was not usable. I have sinned many times, now, then, and in the future. Yet the Lord still loved me. He deserves all the credit for anything good that I might do.

I will never understand why he chose me unless, as my Lord loved David, he also loved me.

Acts 13:22 And when he had removed him he raise up unto them David to be their King to who he gave testimony, and said I have found, David the son of Jese, a man after mine own heart, who shall fulfill, all my will:

and...

Romans 5:8: "But God commendeth his love toward us in that, while we were yet sinners, Christ died for us."

Jesus gave his life for **ME**. Make it personal. He died for me before the foundation of the world. He died for me while I was a sinner, unlovable. I was not lovable, but he still loved me. I cannot comprehend why God loved me in the past, present, or future. But like David, I have always had the feeling inside, no matter how far I stayed away, that the Lord keeps telling me, Morris, you are a <u>Man of my own heart</u>; I do not understand this. It is too huge of a concept for me to get my mind around. Please do not think I believe I am a David here. That is not the point. The point is that the Lord used David in an excellent way for the future, as he was preparing David, as a Shepherd keeping his sheep, becoming the King of Israel, and insuring the bloodline from Abram to Jesus, which was prophesized.

God already knew the sins that David would commit in the future. God hoped that David would not sin, but in his foreknowledge, he knew he would. David exercised his free will as we all do. God loved him anyway, although David, you, and I make terrible messes of our lives.

Thank God for the blood of Jesus, who cleanses us and blots out our sins so that our God can look upon us, even though we have sinned and will continue to sin even after he has died for us on the cross.

> *Romans 5: V.8-9: But God commendeth his love toward us in that, while we were yet sinners, Christ died for us. V.9: Much more than; being now justified by his blood, we shall be saved from wrath through him.*

The Lord still considered David a man of God's own heart and always loved him and directed him, although God already knew that David would fail him. I believe that refers to the repentant heart that David had. When David sinned, his repentance and faith in God returned even after he had lost the battles of the flesh. Take the time to read the Book of Palms and the other writings of David. David tore off his clothes in shame when he was sorry for his sins and repented.

> *Romans 5: V. 16: and not as it was by one that shinned, so is the gift; for the judgment was by one to condemnation, but the free gift is of many offenses unto justification.*

If you have not asked my Lord to save you or are unsure about your salvation, now is an excellent time to surrender your heart to my Lord. All you have to do is ask him, and he will. First, realize you are a sinner, tell the Lord that you are, ask the Lord to forgive you, and enter your heart, mind, and soul. Then believe he has accepted you into his flock.

That is why I believe it is such a shame when a preacher uses the pulpit to badger his flock, forgetting that he is only a for-given sinner, anointed by God, saved by the mercy of God, and just like David, you, me, and those also in his flock. The Shepherd is there to have compassion as Jesus always did, and be firm and tell the truth, but let Gods' word convict someone's mind and soul. No personal attacks. Again, back to Brother Babb, "Morris, You cannot legislate Righteousness," only God can change the heart.

Romans 2:1 "Therefore thou art inexcusable, O man, whosoever thou art that judgest: for wherein thou judgest another, thou condemnest thyself: for thou that judgest doest the same things.

Judge not, or you will be judged by the same judgment (the same tone, and compassion, and details you used to make your judgment and condemn others) you will be judged by. I do not know about you, but I need all the forgiveness I can get in my life. I am up to the 77 times, 7.

Matthew 18:V.21-22 Then came to Peter to him came into him and said, Lord, how often shall my brother sin against me, and I forgive him?

Till seven times- V. 22 Jesus saith unto him, I say not unto thee, Until seven times: but Until seventy time seven.

(Jesus teaches us to forgive) times, 1,000,000, or every time. I hope and pray for understanding and compassion when I am judged at the Judgment seat of Christ.

This is the time you would say do as I say to do, not what I doeth.

Romans 7:16: "If then, I do that which I would not, I consent unto the Law this it is good. V.17: No, then it is no more I that do it, but the sin that dwelleth in me.

As Paul says, I do what I know, not to do. I do not understand why. I know better, but I do it anyway; we all do. Therefore, it is not I that doeth it, but the Sin which lives within me.

Thank God for Jesus, who has already forgiven me, David, and you for every sin you and I have committed and will commit in the future. God forgave us even before the foundation of the world. He had already paid the price in God's mind or spirit. All we have to do is to believe, understand only by faith is it possible.

> *John 1: V. 1: In the beginning was the Word, and the Word was with God, and the Word was God. V.2. The same was in the beginning with God. V. 3. All thighs were made by him; and without him was not anything made that was made.*

I worked in construction building homes while I was in college:

While going to college, I worked for a small construction business. It was a tiny business. Therefore, the owner, Mr. Jernigan, and his son Buddy did most of the work. Consequently, I learned all types of construction, framing, roofing, tie beams and poring floors, and much more. When I went away to a two-year Jr. College and senior years at Fla. Atlantic, I continued to make my way by working weekends in the construction industry. It made me enough income to go to college with my wonderful and dear high School sweetheart, Linda, my wife, today of over 53 years. I made a lot of revenue back then. I average well over 100.00 per day, which was a lot then.

I majored in Distributive Education in College, not English, which would help me run multiple businesses and become a building contractor. I studied marketing, advertising, management, accounting, business law, economics, and more. These courses aided me in starting a large hardware store business in Immokalee with a partner's help. I am trying to point out that I did not understand that I would need this knowledge and experience in the Church's building. I had no idea at the time that God was directing my path, so I would be prepared to be used by him for his Glory in the plans he had for me.

Remember, I should not have been able to go to college. However, in the construction business, hardware business, my past experiences in the business world gave me the confidence to build the new Church, building ourselves, saving 100s of 1000s, which we did, later in this true story.

Later I built several homes and ran a few commercial building projects in Immokalee. I also became a 50% owner of B & L Hardware, Seafood Market, and rental business in the Florida Keys, building contractor, and other business ventures.

New Church Shepherd: Bother Larry Finely called as Pastor in 1982, a new area begins:

A new era began at the First Baptist Church in the old building in the old town Immokalee. The new Pastor brought youth, energy, leadership, direction, purpose, and vision into the Church. He is the best Bible scholar I have ever had the privilege of listening to. He knew the word and encouraged and motivated others to study it. From the very beginning, before the Church called him, he stated that the Lord had sent him to First Baptist of Immokalee to build a new church facility. The facility on the property was set aside by others years ago. When the pulpit committee interviewed him, he told them God called him to Immokalee build on the property. Brother Babb and I call it the Promised Land.

First by adding to the numbers of the Church and second, the Lord had given him a vision that the Lord wanted a new Church facility on the property located in the center of the new town, which Robert's family donated to the Church. I called this the Promised Land.

Brother Larry was an excellent Shepard and at the head of his flock leading from the front, not trailing behind them. He led by example, with vision and purpose, visiting everyone he could. He set aside one evening a week for a visitation program to visit the physically ill and spiritually ill. He encouraged all members to participate. He started and would come to Thursday night church visitation even when no others showed up to go with him. Pretty soon, others began to arrive. He was a leader and used his witness to motivate others to participate. He did not just talk about it. He walked the walk. He put his feet into his prayer

He also encouraged and believed in a strong deacon body. He seeks out other Godly servants with many different talents to help him. I cannot remember any other time in the Churches history when the Church had so many deacons. This body of Godly men had unbelievable faith and encouragement, supporting the vote to build the facility on the Promised Land.

Because of Brother Larry's youthful energy and devotion to do what he thought was why the Lord led him to the Church, he kept on track. He gave the church a purpose to exist, reaching the lost.

He had a big impression on my heart for his love for the lost. He had such a burden for the lost. His commitment and love for the lost influenced me so much that we became partners at the beginning of visitation as we were sent out two by two as Jesus sent out his disciples. We did one on one soul-winning many times. The first of which was a man named Brown Thompson who was bedridden. What an experience that was.

The Lord impressed on my heart Brother Larry's love for the lost. The Lord blessed a visitation program that he had laid upon my heart. The Church appointed me as the visitation director. Before long, we had almost all the deacons and others going out on visitation every Thursday night.

The Lord used this program to have 125 souls accept Jesus in one year. The Lord had prepared so many hearts for us to visit that we even had to have invitations for the profession of faith on Wednesday night services. This significant increase in numbers was one of the motivations why we needed a larger church facility.

I love and respected brother Larry then, now, and forever. But we all have our faults, shorting comings and none are perfect. As for me, I have thousand of flaws and shortcomings. In my mind, Brother Larry was a bit too legalistic while he was at First Baptist in Immokalee. We have talked about this. I only mention this not to hurt or dig at Brother Larry, but to make a point of reference to others and myself to be careful as Brother Babb told me we could not legislate righteousness. That, in the end, trying legislating morality will turn people away.

Again, I love and respect Brother Larry, who had the most extraordinary Christian influence on my life. The Lord encourages me to build the new facility, but Brother Larry, to be given credit. Without his impact on my Christian life, I do not believe I would have come as close to my Lord as I did during his ministry.

He was young and lacked many experiences in life, just like me at that time. As you get older, you realize that life experience really can't be taught but experienced through life's trials. He came across sometimes as if you should do something, just because the Bible teaches it, which is right and best for us, but too much law, legalistic, and not enough love and compassion. We should do for our Lord because we love him.

I only bring this up to point out another point later in this story. After Brother Larry's ministry was completed, Brother Daryl Alexander was our next pastor, who had the most compassion for people I have ever witnessed. Brother Larry was what we needed in our Church at that time in our history. It also goes back to the point I continue to make in this story. God knows best what we need and will give us our needs and sometimes our wants if we genuinely seek his will.

It is essential when a Church is choosing its spiritual leader. Later in this true story, the Lord again sends us the exact person we need, full of compassion and love, after the foundations set for the building project. But, unfortunately, Brother Larry decides that his mission is completed and moves to a different church before construction starts.

We should do things for our Lord because we love him and appreciate what he did for you and me on the cross. Remember, all those stripes of the whip were supposed to be for us/me. Jesus took our place on the cross. Always remember he took my/your place on the cross. It should have been us nailed to the cross. We are the ones who sinned. Jesus was perfect without sin. Always make it personal, and you will begin to comprehend what Jesus has done for us. Quite frankly, I would NOT have died for you, even if I liked you. But Jesus died for you and ME, even when you and I were sinners. He died for us, knowing that we would sin and continue in sin.

> *John 19:V1 Then Pilate, therefore, took Jesus and scourged him. John 19:V17 And he, bearing his cross, went forth into a place called the place of a skull, which is called in the Hebrew Golgotha. John 19: V23 Then the soldiers, when they had crucified Jesus.*

The lack of compassion or ability to express those truths with love is where I believe many Shepherds miss the mark, especially in 2013. Condemning without mercy from the pulpit, Brother Larry never did this. He never did this in public or

87

personal attacks from the pulpit. Personal attacks are not from our Lord. I believe the flesh and pride control us when personal attacks happen.

He is still a dear friend, and I love him, and he did make a big difference in my life and many others. He continued to build upon Brother Babb Adams's foundation before him. I have expressed my thoughts with him a few times over the past years, and we believe we both have grown and matured in many different ways. However, I still consider him the best teacher/preacher/pastor I have ever known. I would love to hear him preach/teach the word again. I would love for him to be my pastor again.

The only reason I put this part into this true story is that those who knew him could have some insight into the great work that he and Brother Babb Adams both did in Immokalee. In building the new Church Building, the Body of Christ, and influencing the people, God prepared to develop his New Church Building for many years.

I believe it was planned before the foundation of the world, since we have an all-knowing and all-seeing God who sees the future, before He and the Word created the world and knew that he would let his only Son, Jesus, go to the Cross for all our sins.

> *Ephesians 1: 4: According as he hath chosen us in him before the foundation of the world, that we should be holy and without blame before him in love. V5: Having predestinated us unto*

the adoption of sons by Jesus Christ to himself according to the good pleasure of his will.

The concept of building a new facility started close to 100 years before. During my role in the Church, Brother Babb Adams and Brother Larry Finley, I believe all the events were in God's plan to build his Church. Brother Babb Adams carried on the idea and laid the foundation, of course, with the help of others, so it would be possible to build our Lord's new facility. Like Mosses, Brother Larry was the catalyzer to get the building started, like Joshua. From the beginning of his ministry and even before Brother Larry was accepted as the new pastor, he stated that God sent him to Immokalee to build a new facility. To build it on the land that Brother Babb and others had secured. It would become a shining light in the center of the town of Immokalee. All those who travel to or through Immokalee would see.

The Beginning of the Dream/ Idea of a new Church Building:

I have written a lot of history that may not be of interest to anyone. Nevertheless, I felt it essential and compelled to write about some of the past. It should help others better understand how building a new church building started. First, I believe we all must look back into history to appreciate what others have done before us. And second, so we will not make the same mistakes repeatedly.

It was a **MIRACLE** to get 100s of Baptist members to agree to do something and shuffle our way through all the mummers and constant common issues in most churches. Remember, it is called a Church, family. Think about your own family and the trials, errors, and turmoil that your own family goes through in life, especially in today's world. Satan knows his time is short.

> *Revelation: V11-16 and I saw heaven opened and behold a white horse, and he that sat upon him was called Faithful and True, and in righteousness, he doth judge and make war.*

I do not believe that in today's world, 2013 and 2020, it would have been possible to build the church building if we had not done it on God's timetable. The main reason is the unity in a Church. Second, it is much more complicated today with all the new regulations, zoning and building codes, and impact fees. It would cost millions more to replace the present church building, even if it were a much smaller church facility.

Brother Larry continues to confirm that the Lord has led him to Immokalee to build a new Church on the Promised Land:

Brother Larry was convinced in his heart that it was time to build a new church facility. After all that year, in 1985, 125 were saved and joined the church in the old Church facility. It can be done again in 2013 and beyond. God is still in the **SAVING** business.

A Baptist Church is pretty much a complete democracy. It is not an efficient way to do a construction project, with 250 bosses, many with different ideas and opinions.

My Lord started working on my mind and heart. First, my Lord convinced me that he had been preparing me all my life for the task of building his Church on the Promised Land. Then, he directed the path in my life's journey to acquire experience as a building contractor, hardware store owner, and businessman.

My pastor was convinced that the Lord wanted it built. I believe my pastor and the Lord spoke to my mind and heart about constructing a new facility. Our numbers were growing, and we needed more room for all the new people coming to our church.

Our present facility was filling up. It made sense rather than remolded to build a new facility. After the was land free and clear already, I believed we could sell the older facility, which has served its purpose for many years. It was in the center of the older section of the town. It was valuable, and it should sell quickly. These funds could be used toward paying off construction loans and mortgages.

At this time in history, we had the exact people needed with the precise talents required to build the new Church building:

We also had the exact people in our church who we needed to do this massive project. I always thought of them as the total body members, the arms, legs, feet, brains, ideas. They had many different talents that would be needed and helpful in building a new facility.

God gathered all the needed talents to build his new church and already had placed them in his Church (ANOTHER MIRACLE). The chances of having the exact people you needed to create a new facility were not by accident. I believed our Lord planned it. Anyone who thought, in 2013, that it was going to be easy to build a new church building if they sold the Promised Land is sadly mistaken.

This is one reason I went into so much history and details of all the events in the past. This history should give the Church of 2013, which was considering selling the Promised Land, insight into how difficult it would be.

Considering building a new facility could split the Church. In 2013 some of the Church's leadership decided that it was best to sell the property and build a much smaller Church.

I began checking on some details in 2013 and came to an unmistakable and quick conclusion that there was no anyway the church could afford to have a contractor build the new building. The square footage cost estimates were ridiculous, even in the 1980s. God had given us all the talents we needed in our church body. All we had to do was to organize and someone to lead them.

I cannot imagine the total cost in today's market. I would guess 7-8 million to replace buildings and land in 2013. There was some talk about selling the property for only 4 million by church leaders in 2013. We built the two buildings for about 400K. There were also many other kinds and types of dominations. One example written about later in this story was 50K Miracle in fill dirt donated for the building's foundation. Jack Queen was one of those members that God had already placed in his Church in his foreknowledge. There were many others.

The Lord had placed a building floor plan in my mind. It was simple and very cost-effective to build. However, can you imagine how much time would be needed to get a Church agreement on drafting the plans? It was a miracle that we all decided in 1985 in a unified Church. How much more difficult would it be in 2013 with a divided Church.

The design gave us all the classrooms we needed and many other things that the old church building did not have. In addition, it included a Family Life Center, a substantial professional kitchen, and a gym, with a high school regulation basketball court, which could be used to reach the youth for our Lord.

I could not understand why the Church of 2013 was considering building a smaller facility? The false reasoning was that church attendance was down, and the facility's upkeep was too expensive. I did not believe that if a new smaller facility were built, it would solve the issues of low attendance, poor maintenance, and lack of income.

The first construction committee meeting was not successful in 1984:

We called for a meeting of the whole church of anyone interested in building a new facility. I will never forget that meeting, as long as I live. I believe there were at least 50 people at the conference. I laid out my plan to build the church, build ourselves, and save 100s of 1000s. First, of course, we would hire a project manager and pay a contractor's fee to pull the permits. So here I am, at the front, explaining the plan. Brother Larry was in a chair in the front row on the right side. There were 50 or more people at the meeting. Most of these people I had not been in church in years. They started asking question after question, tearing the plan apart. They continually said it could not be done. We have to do this or that before getting permits. It was an impossible plan. The mountains were too high.

> *Numbers 13:1-33: V1 And the Lord spoke unto Moses, saying.V2 Send thou men, that they may search the Land of Canaan, which <u>I give unto the children of Israel</u>: of every tribe (12 tribes 12 men) of their fathers shall ye send a man, every one a ruler among them. V27 and they told him and said, we came unto the land to which thou sentest us and surely it floweth with milk and honey: V 30 And caleb, <u>stilled</u> the people, before Moses, and said Let <u>us go up at once and posses it</u>, For we are well able to overcome it. V31 But the men that were with him said, We are not able to go up against the people: for they are stronger than*

we are. V32. And they brought up an evil report of the land. V33. And there we saw the giants, the sons of Anak we were in our own sight as grasshoppers

Charter 14 V 2. And all the children of Israel murmured against Moses and against Aaron. V6. (only two of the 12 spies believed and trusted God that they could take the Promised Land. 1984 build the new church facility) And Joshua, the son of Nun, and Caleb, the son Jephun'neh, who were of them that searched the land. V7 and they spoke unto all the company (the Church members in the room) Saying The Land (New Church building) is good. V 8: If the Lord delight in us, then he will bring us into this land, and give it to us. V 10. But all the congregation demanded to stone them with stones. (We cannot do it. Forget this terrible plan.) (Stones/angry words were thrown at the messenger)

The mountains/obstacles were too high/significant. Still, I believed nothing is impossible for our Lord: Like Mosses, who sent the 12 spies into their promised land when they gave their report, there were many doubters and negative comments. The army in the "Promised Land" was massive and could not be defeated. Some giants lived in the "Promised Land." I cannot recall any positive comments that we can do all things through Christ who strengthens us. I believe that an unfaithful army cannot do anything for our Lord. It is impossible to please God without faith. In that room that day, the people were overwhelming against my Lord and me.

Matthew 21:V21: Verily I say unto you, If ye have faith and doubt not, ye shall not only, do this which is done to the fig tree, but also, if ye shall say unto this mountain, Be thou removed, and be thou cast into the sea, it shall be done.

The spies could only see the enemies/problems/obstacles/ which held/lived the Promise Land. They said there were too many modern weapons that could destroy us, and on and on. Like the Children of Israel, (10 of the 12 spies sent out gave adverse reports. Most did not believe Mosses that God had told him that the Promised Land was at was theirs. Those in the room used every negative reason not to go into the "Promised Land" and build a larger modern Church, which God had promised them.

Even Brother Larry, at that point, seemed to me to lose his faith and vision and started doubting. He did not stand with me. He understood that we could do all things through Christ Jesus, who strengthens us. We all have our weak moments when our faith leaves us. I sure have had my lack of faith moments in my own life. The person who I trusted most who had convinced me that God called him to our Church to build a new facility on the Promised Land did not support me. It was a <u>miracle</u> that I did not lose my faith. If God had not spoken directly to my heart at the moment during that meeting, I would have also lost my faith. I did not need all the personal attacks on me. After all, I had different businesses to run and manage. It would be much easier for me to agree.

> *Philippians 4:13 I can do all things through Christ, who strengtheneth me and V. 19: But my God shall supply all your need according to his riches in glory by Jesus Christ.*

I kept trying to explain to them that we could build it. God could do anything. Nothing is impossible with God. I pointed out that we had the exact talents within our Church body to complete the project. I pointed out that we could not afford to build it if we did not build it ourselves. I pointed out that if we did not build it now, we might never have the same opportunity to build it. I did this over and over for about 30 minutes.

> *Matthew 19: V. 26: With men, this is impossible, but with God, all things are possible.*

I knew that because of my vast building and business experience, the Lord had already prepared me for this task, really my entire life. I knew we could build it. I had already done it before in my own life when I built my home and other building projects.

I had complete faith that IT WAS God's Will to begin this building process idea and layout. I discussed and argued with the group for, I guess, about ½ hour. Then, all of a <u>sudden, the Lord spoke directly to my heart, as clear as a bell</u>. **"<u>MORRIS FORGET IT</u>,"** just like the children of Israel, who sent 12 spies into the promised land and only 2, when they gave their report, believed they could take the "Promised Land" that I gave them. So I gave them up and made them wander for forty years. In their future, they would come back to the same place they could have taken 40 years before". **<u>Stop! Resign, from the Committee, this minute</u>.**

> *Numbers 14:11 And the Lord said unto Moses, How long will these people provoke me? And how long will it be before they Believe me, for all the signs which I have shown among them. V23 Surely they shall not see the land which I swore to give unto their fathers, (the early church leaders, men of faith, and filled with the Holy Spirit, at the First Baptist Church of Immokalee, believed the in the promise that a new Church building in the heart of Immokalee, and were lead by God to locate the "Promise Land" Hwy 29 and Lake Trafford) neither shall any of them that provoked see it. Those who have ears let them hear. Then the children of Israel wandered for another 40 years.*

Thank God that he did not make the First Baptist Church wait for another 40 years before building a new facility on the Promised Land. It was delayed. But later, it out worked for good, as all things do if we wait on God and lean not on our understanding. It is an essential lesson for us all to learn in life. I am not sure I have learned that lesson or not in my own life. Hopefully, this book will help others learn to trust God and lean on Him and not themselves. This theme is throughout this book.

Will the Promised Land be delayed for another 40 years? Will the First Baptist Church wonder in the wildness?

Therefore, that is what I did to everyone's surprise. I resigned as chairmen before the meeting was over. However, as I recall, I was the only Spy in the camp/Church construction meeting, which believed we could build the new facility. Sometimes you have to stand alone, but you and God make a Marjory.

Numbers 32:V13 Ad the LORD'S anger was kindled against Israel, and he made them wander in the wilderness forty years, until all the generation that had done evil in the sight of the LORD was consumed

I wish there had been another spy with me, which also had the faith and believed we could build the church, but really at that time, it would not have made any difference. There was too much doubt in the room.

This brings out another important principle: sometimes God wants you to take a stand in faith, even if you are all alone. This is what a small raiment of church members did in 2013. In 2013, many members were deceived into believing the Promised Land should be sold. This fact is one reason God compelled me to write the Journey to the Promised Land story. If they read about the Miracles during the facility's construction, it would encourage them to stand against the sale.

There may only be one of only a few who understands the will of God. Many times in life, only a few listen to God's will and have the faith necessary to continue the race. Like the Old Testament prophets speaking to the Kings of that day and warning them, they were out of God's will. They were placing their very lives on the line. Who has ears to hear, let him hear?

It is a hard thing to do. The flock or the King does not always know what is best for the herd. Sometimes even the Sheppard loses their way and faith. Read the story in your Bible about David and Saul. God always has someone to stand for him in faith. Consider the prophets in the Old Testament.

I often have wondered what Moses said to those who did not believe they could take the "Promised Land." He was in the meeting when 10 of the 12 spies said, "the land could not be taken." I assume that he could not convince the Children of Israel even after they had witnessed all the **MIRACLES** that God had performed for them on their Journey from Egypt headed to the Promised Land. What about the **MIRACLES** that happened before they were released from Egypt?

Whatever he said was not enough to convince the flock that they could take the "Promised Land." You should read the story in the Bible of all the **MIRACLES** God did for Israel. They were seeable and touchable. For example, he fed them with manna from Heaven. God did not even let Mosses enter the Promised Land. He let Joshua take the Promised Land. Joshua believed God that they could take the promised land. Brother Larry was shocked that I resigned from my construction committee chairmanship role. Now our Church had no one in a leadership role for the construction of the new building. All progress stopped. There were not any plans for moving forward. I believe this attitude continued for months. But God had a different plan shortly for those of little faith. Thank God for his love, long-suffering, and patience toward us. It is a good thing I was not God because I would have given them up to wonder in their misery.

A physical, touchable, seeable <u>MIRACLE</u>: The finding of my God-given design layout building, already built.

Months passed, and I was also in the construction business at that time. We always put a new sign-up on our new building projects. We were fixing to start a new project, and I had to go to Fort Myers and pick up the new job site sign.

My wife was beside me in our truck on this day. She can testify to these facts because she remembers that day very well. I always used a specific route to go pick up the sign. We had used that route many times before, over the old Edison Bridge. They had built a new bridge, which I had never used before. I knew it would take me to the same place. The bridges are about 5 miles apart. I knew the new bridge would take me to the same place if I turned west. I had to cut across to get them where I was going, only a few miles out of my way if any.

One of many Miracles while on the Journey to the "Promised Land."The Lord will direct your path if you will listen and hear him:

I was very close to the Lord in those days. The <u>Lord spoke directly</u> again to me in my truck while driving. **"<u>MORRIS, I WANT YOU TO GO THIS NEW WAY TO GET YOUR SIGN</u>."** I am telling you the complete truth, even if you do not believe me, and I told my wife at that instant, **"<u>Doll, the Lord just told me to go a different route to pick up the sign</u>."**

This is a picture of the bridge that we went over when the Lord spoke to me to take a different route that I had never used before.

It was as if another person, my Lord's spirit or his angel, was sitting beside me and between us in the truck. He spoke to me clear as a bell. My wife and I talk about this miracle often.

> *Proverbs 3:V. 5-6: Trust in the Lord with all thine heart, and lean not onto thine own understanding. V.6 In all thy ways acknowledge him, and he shall direct thy paths.*

I was driving, and my wife was on the passenger's side of my truck. Jesus's spirit or his Angel was in the middle of both of us in the front seat. I had no reason to go that way, except I knew the Lord told me to. At that point, I did not know why. I thought it was to avoid a tragedy on the old route. I had heard stories of some who were supposed to get on planes and did not since the Lord told them to wait or delay them, and later that plane crashed. Later after 911, I talked to two different people who said they were supposed to be in that building, but God changed their paths for some reason changed their courses.

I had to make a definite choice. Often, I/we do not listen to our Lord and go down the wrong paths. But this time, I decided to go the new route. I knew the Lord had spoken to me. I did not have any idea why I was supposed to take this different route. Many people have to make definite choices at other points in their lives. Always try your best to listen to what your Lord says. He will always lead you to the correct path or road of life for your best.

> *Exodus 14V 13: And Moses said unto the people, Fear Not, Stand Still, and see the salvation of the LORD which he will show to you today; for the Egyptians whom ye have seen today, ye shall see them again no more forever.*

I strongly suggest that you pray about your choices and listen to the still soft voice of our Lord and Savior. If I had not heard that voice, I believe we may not have had the church building or, at a minimum, it would have been delayed, and we would have been still wondering for many more months or years. It would be months before I would have any reason to take this particular route. It was indeed a **MIRACLE** that I took this new route; please believe me. Words cannot explain those moments when my Lord or an angel was sitting beside us in the truck.

Remember, it was not normal for me to take the new route. <u>I had to choose, and many others have to make choices in the trials through life</u>. Some have to decide to accept my Lord as their savior and Lord of their life. Always trust in your Lord, and he will guide you in the right direction. They are easy words to say but very hard to live. Some will preach that it is an easy road, but it is not. You need to be aware of the cost of following Jesus. There are always ups and downs, and we still have to fight off Satan's fiery darts. But once you get to your final destination, you will be glad you chose the correct route in life.

But my Lord cannot hear you unless you are his child. It is similar in human life; rarely will a child ask another father for something. That child will only ask his father. So the only prayer/petition that my Lord can hear from a person who does not know him, a lost person head to Hell, is that person asking for forgiveness and asking Jesus to live inside of him. Once God becomes your heavenly father, he can hear our prayer/requests/petition.

But once you are a child of God, you may talk to him as you would your earthly father, but of course, with more reverence. If you are talking to the United States President, you will honor and respect him. You are now talking directly with the creator of the universe. An assume God who loves you enough to send his son to die in your place while we were sinners, on the cross so that we could have a relationship with him.

> *Matthew 7: V. 11 If ye then, being evil, know how to give good gifts*

> *Matthew 7: V. 11 If ye then, being evil, know how to give good gifts unto your children, how much more shall your Father, who is in heaven, give good things to them that ask him.*

My Lord gave me the insight to choose the right road for me to travel down:

We traveled down that road until we got to the turnoff and turned west within minutes, which would take us to where the sign was to be a pickup. I saw a new building designed by the Lord's direction, just like the one I had made a rough draft drawing of. I told my wife I needed to stop and talk to someone here. I needed to take a look at this building. I mentioned to her; I knew now why the Lord led us down this road instead of the old route we always had taken.

This is a picture taken in 2020 of the Church building I saw in 1984. It was almost completed. After turning on a road that I had never traveled before, I saw it. The first covered entrance to the right is where Brother Bobby Jones was laying the title. It is the location where I first meet him.

After we turned and traveled a few miles down the road, we saw a building already completed, almost exactly like the one we already had a rough draft of. Brother Bobby Jones was laying the tile on the walkway up to the building side door.

I parked my truck and walked up to the entrance, and I saw a giant of a man. I remember thinking this was like David and Goliath. I am 5'4," and he looked to be over 7 feet tall. He was a broad and very husky man. He was laying tile at the front entrance. I introduced myself and shook his hand, he broke mine with his grip, and he said, "I am Brother Bobby Jones, and this is our church."

We began talking, and he told me that he was the church's pastor. He also said to me that the Church was building this church themselves. He was a good listener, gentle, and easy to talk to. Nothing like the giant I thought he was. We talked for about an hour. I told him the story of how the Lord put into my mind almost the same layout for a church Immokalee. I could tell he believed me and my story. I think the Spirit of my Lord had already prepared him for me to show up. We discussed how he handled the building process and his procedures to get the building process started. He told me about the 1000s of 1000s his church had saved by not using a building contractor. Also, how they could build it themselves. The building was almost a carbon copy of what I had told our pastor, Brother Larry, and the church construction meeting months ago. The building was also the exact match of the church's basic design I had drafted on paper months before.

I started thinking about the construction committee meeting a few months ago that was determined that we could not build. That only 30 miles away, there was a building almost exactly like the layout God had given met in the finishing stages.

This picture taken in 2020 is of the front entrance of the Church, which Brother Bobby Jones Church built-in 1984. Latter images will point how that it matches the entrance of the First Baptist Church finished in 1986.

God had to have known that the structure had already begun and was almost completed. I, of course, did not know. He revealed this only after the Church building was nearly 100% complete. What if I had taken this route months ago before, during the beginning construction process? I would have only seen the foundation. I would not have even noticed the project. <u>I know God had the timing planned to the exact moment</u>. What do you think? Is there any other possible explanation? I know that it was a **<u>MIRACLE</u>**. There is no further reasonable explanation! But wait, the Miracles get even better as this story continues.

Now, I wondered why the Lord had not revealed the construction project's existence to me months before I resigned from the Church's construction committee as chairman. We could have seen the construction in the beginning process months ago. I believe it was because God, in His wisdom, knew the timing was not suitable for several reasons. <u>First,</u> which was the lack of faith of so many in our Church, I believe that even if they had known about the other Church almost exactly like my actual dawning, they still would not have thought we could build it ourselves.

God always knows in his perfect wisdom what we need and when to reveal it to us. Just like he reveals to us today what is in the book of Revelation, he knew that the doubters would need to see the almost finished product before they would believe. He knows that we could not understand the book of Revelation until the last days in his wisdom. This is why he is now revealing it to us.

<u>Second,</u> I also believe that God knew that the original course I was taking with the construction committee would not have worked. He knew that too many people, there would be too many Chiefs. There would be too many different positions, ideas, and plans to make the construction impossible. I also realized this, and is why I only had five members when I set up the new construction committee. They had to believe in the project. They must be willing to commit to doing anything to help the construction project.

There are no other logical reasons to explain the events and specific paths, except the word **Miracle**. How can you not believe that our Lord did not have this all planned out? It did not just happen by chance what a **MIRACLE** to find the same basic layout of a church, already constructed, by those building it by themselves. You that have ears listen and hear the Lord speaking to your heart.

Why would I have taken a road that I was unfamiliar with and never used before to pick up a business sign? Why would I not use the same route that I had used many times before? It could not have been an accident for me to drive by the Lord's design's exact church layout. It could not have just been an accident for me to have walked up at the precise moment that the pastor of that church was finishing up laying the tile in the front entrance. It was not an accident for the pastor to be there. It was not by accident to meet the pastor during the finishing stages of construction. There were just too many accidents or variables to say it happened by chance.

Consider, what if I had not listened to my Lord on the road (LIFE'S PATH, the journey) before, and made the right decision of which route (path of life) that God wanted me to take? Our daily choices in choosing the suitable courses for our journey through life should always include our Lord in them. If we listen to our Lord's direction, he will guide our paths and give us abundant life and the "PROMISED LAND."

What if I had delayed this trip and had not gone down the right path the Lord wanted me to travel? What if I had chosen a different day to go pick up the sign? What if I had gone down the other bridge my old route (the wrong decision) or came back through the new road later on my way around? Would Brother Bobby still have been there to meet me, or would he have finished his tile work and been off the project grounds?

Timing is critical with God; if you miss the timing in his overall plan, you might miss the best of the blessing in your Journey to your "Promised Land." So the exact timing of all these little advents would have had to be perfect for me to have arrived on the right day and time. So it is safe to say it was not by accident but a **MIRACLE**.

It was not just quiescence. It defiantly was A **Miracle** on our Journey to the Promised Land.

Brother Bobby Jones, another "Miracle," meets with Brother Larry at his new church facility in North Fort Myers. Brother Larry sees the Church facility that matches precisely the layout that the Lord had given me already completed:

I asked Brother Bobby Jones to meet with Brother Larry and me. I wanted him to explain how we could build our Church. Brother Bobby was in the final stages of finishing his project. Brother Bobby showed the facility to Brother Larry. We could see it and touch it. Since the information was coming from another pastor that was building the facility by themselves, it was more believable. It was easy now to believe what he was saying was true; we could see the results. It did not take a lot of faith to believe now. We could see the physical evidence and touch it. We visited and went inside the almost completed Church building of Brother Bobby's.

This strengthened Brother Larry's faith and renewed his belief/call that the Lord led him to Immokalee to build his new Church faculty. He had never lost the desire or hope. It was just dimed for a while.

Remember Brother Larry, when I stood up in the first Construction meeting months before the Children of Israel, the Church crowd did not support me. The fact that we could build the new church building ourselves. He had listened to some of the doubting spies who believed we couldn't build it. We need to be careful of who listens to man or God!

I would not say that his faith and belief were gone but weakened. He had some doubts that we or I could do what the Lord had convinced me that we could do. It is impossible to please God without faith.

> *Bible verse it is impossible to please God without faith Matthew 17: V 20 And Jesus said unto them, Because of your unbelief; for verily I say unto you, If ye have faith as a grain of mustard seed, ye shall say unto this mountain, Move from here to younder place, and it shall move, and nothing shall be impossible unto you*

Brother Bobby Jones answered many of the doubters' questions and the ten doubting spies at the original Construction meeting. He had all the answers to those concerned over the church members completing the building project independently. The exact timing of all these events lining up, 1,2,3, makes it impossible for me to believe that it just happened by chance. As I told the church members at that time, anyone who thought these events were an accident is of little

Faith and has little understanding of how our Lord works in our daily lives. You that have ears listen and hear the Lord speaking to your heart. I know it was a **MIRACLE**, but only one of many I will write about as I continue this long true story on the Journey to the Promised Land.

I believed that the First Baptist Church body of 2013 needed to understand the Churches history, the Journey, and the especially MIRACLES that happen. Then, when it was time to consider selling or not selling "The Promised Land," they would make the right decision.

In 1985 when we were considering building a new facility, we needed something to grab hold of to strengthen our faith. God provided exactly what we needed. I hope this book will also inspire the Church of 2013 and increase their faith and insight in making the right decision concerning selling the Promised Land. After reading this book, the 2013 church members will hopefully understand by reading and remembering the Miracles of what God had already done in the process of reaching the Promised Land in 1985. The fact that there was a church only 30 miles away precisely like the one we discussed already built and was the final faith builder we needed to renew our faith.

I hoped that once the members were reminded and some became knowledgeable for the first time that God himself caused the **MIRACLES** written about in this book, they would understand that the Promised Land was a unique Holly ground that should not be destroyed or sold.

Knowing that God had directed my path to the already built facility renewed my faith made it even more potent, and I was compelled to share it with others. I am the only one who could tell this entire story who witnessed and understood that the events were **MIRACLES** if we could have only had the faith of a mustard seed! But now, they did not need faith because we could all see what God had already done.

This story is a lot more than just the building of Church building. It should be apparent to anyone reading it that it also gives an insight into how the Lord works in our daily lives. That if we listen to his still soft voice, he will lead us and guide us through the trails, broken hearts, and turmoil of life. In the end, we will arrive at our "Promised Land." The road is narrow, and unfortunately, only a few will choose the right road.

> *Matthew 7: V. 13-14 Enter in at the narrow gate, for wide is the gate, and broad is the way, that leadeth to destruction, and many there be who go in that way: Because narrow is the gate and hard is the way, which leadeth unto life, and few there that find it.*

I remember all the Miracles that happened in the process of building the Church as if they had happened today:

The **Miracle** of me **overhearing** my wife's sister Karen's phone call to her when I was over 20 feet away and still hearing what was said concerning the vote to sell the Promised Land was written about earlier in this book. This fact began the urgency for the completion of this book.

As I continue to write this true story, I continually pray the Lord will guide my hand and mind. The Lord has kept it fresh for many years, and I can see these details as if it was happening today. Yet, there are hundreds of things and people I can no longer remember. You that have ears listen and hear the Lord speaking to your heart. I know this is another **MIRACLE, the of remembering the details**.

When you get older, you get much wiser, But your mind gets and starts putting its files in the archive folders. So I have forgotten many things, places, and people. But the details of this Journey will always stay clear in my mind, which is a Miracle in itself. I keep seeing them over and over as if they were happening live at this moment.

My wife, Linda, continues to say, "don't you remember this or that" about our children and other vital events in our life. I have to say honestly, no many times. But this true story is clear as a bell in my mind, heart, and soul. The Lord has kept these events and facts clearly in my mind for a reason. It brings tears to my eyes still today as I recall and tell others about the many **MIRACLES** I witnessed.

I do not know how to get a book published yet. There is a war inside me, wondering and doubting if my ego or father will continue to revise this book in 2013 and seek out a publisher. I have been praying that my Lord will lead me to the right publisher. I must have faith and believe that the Lord will provide me with the right company. I am continually checking the grammar and spelling, and content almost daily. I am waiting on God to direct me to the right publishing company.

I believe that Christians are in for some very rough times in the USA. Christians are already being persecuted and killed for their beliefs elsewhere in the world in 2020. I believe the facts about these real-life, believable Miracles will encourage Christians to get ready and keep faith in the hard times before us. Hopefully, it will kindle reflection in those who read it about miracles that happen in their own lives, which they can grasp hold of. I believe that miracles happen all the time around us, but we fail to recognize them.

With this new armor of faith, we are ready to charge forward:

> *Ephesians 6:V11-17 Put on the whole armor of God that ye may be able to stand against the wiles of the devil. V12 for we wrestle not against flesh and blood, but against principalities, against power, against the rulers of the darkness of this world, against spiritual wickedness in high places.*

Now, Brother Larry was on board and fully committed to this new armor, strengthening my faith. We could build it ourselves. After the experience in the earlier construction meetings, my confidence in the Church's people was gone. I knew we could construct the church ourselves. It was God's will. Too many miracles happened to put us in a position to have been by chance.

I was once wondering how and if we were ever going to build a new church building. But now, I was full of faith, ready to charge forward and take the "Promised Land."

But how should we approach this challenging project? Unfortunately, I do not believe that many have the experience, knowledge, and understanding of how hard it is to get church members to agree on anything. Was there too little faith, backbiting, murmurs, jealousy, and turmoil to complete a massive project like this? Those considering the sale of the Promised Land in 2013 should think about these facts.

My Lord always picks the perfect time: Another "Miracle."

I Believe the Lord had it all planned out, just as he did when he chose the timing of writing his Holy Word, the Bible, in the exact perfect time when the Roman Empire came. The Greek language existed before his disciples and others could write the Bible using precise words in the new testament. Until this time, an exact langue did not exist, with specific detailed words that could so clearly express the word of God.

In the English langue, the word love has only one general meaning. But in Greek, there are specific types of love and different words that have more detailed meaning than just the word love. Therefore, every student of the Bible should have a set of Wuest word studies of Greek.

God's timing is always perfect: Throughout the Bible, specific things had to come to the past before the next step could be taken:

> *2 Samuel 7:V 1: And it came to pass. V; 3 Go do all that is in thine heart: for the LORD is with thee. V:4 And it came to pass that night.*
>
> *V:5 Go and tell my servant, David thus saith the LORD, Shalt thou build me a house for me to dwell in?*

He chose the right time and the right place. Thus, from the beginning of the church in 1913, all events prepared the foundation for building on the Promised Land.

The Church building is much more than a church building story; but is a history of life experiences that teaches us/ me how to deal with the many Church and family life issues. I keep hearing some say it is only a building. I honestly believe God intended this building to be the shining Light in Immokalee and the world. **I Believe** that this particular building located on the Promised Land was essential to our Lord's plan in the future, even Holly/Blessed ground. Brother Babb also believed this.

There were just too many things that had to happen in a 1, 2, 3, definite order to 1,000 to make the First Baptist Church in the center of town a reality, just to have been an accident. Remember the dictionaries' description of a Miracle. If the facility had not been started at this time, it probably would have never been built. I know that souls will continue to be saved in the facility. However, Satan will do anything possible to destroy this Church and this Church faultily.

More **"MIRACLES" that happen on THE JOURNEY TO the Promised Land**.

Brother Larry now convinced we could build, 1985:

Brother Larry was now confident that we could construct the Church Building ourselves. The Lord, I believe, had already been preparing the minds and hearts of the flock. We had the land, the ("Promised Land"), and little money to get the project started. Others had set aside a percentage of the church budget for a new building fund in the past.

Therefore, I decided to take on the massive task of building the Church. I never wanted to use my contractor's license or Construction Company at that time to build the Church. I am sure some thought it was my objective to profit from those not walking in the spirit. You will always have that kind of stuff whenever you try to do anything for our Lord. Brush it off and move forward. I did not even have the proper license to do so. Therefore, I contacted Brother Bobby, who had just com-pleted almost the same building, to hire the same contractor who pulled his permits for the construction and hire him to be the contractor of record. He was only on-site a few times. I also hired Bobby Jones to be the site manager.

I understood at that time; I would have to be the one on the site, making the decisions. But Brother Bobby Jones had just built the almost identical design. It was an excellent decision. Brother Bobby Jones knew the companies to contact for the Sanctuary Beams and many other materials we would need. He had an easy-going personality, was calm, and was very easy to work with. In addition, he had a significant Christian spirit of love, compassion, and understanding.

A completely different building strategy was accepted in 1984- 1985. Compared to what had been considered months before in the original construction committee meeting. Another "Miracle"

Understanding the construction business and the hardware and lumber supply business, which the Lord had, prepared me for many years before we began this big project. At the same time, I managed all these businesses, which, I believe, was in God's overall plan to prepare me for this task. I told Brother Larry that I would take on this vast responsibility under the following conditions, and in my opinion, this is the only way this project could move forward. By now, Brother Larry was full of faith and ready to move forward. I believed the Lord used the first construction meeting to teach me and set the conditions and guidelines for building the project.

It is another illustration of bad things that the Lord uses for good. **Romans 8:28**. The following are the conditions and is the fame work that I set. I believe the Lord gave me the wisdom from my experience. After the experience dealing with the "Children of Israel"(the doubters) in the first construction meetings months ago. The Lord guided me on how to proceed with the building project. Once the Church members, those for the building process and those opposed, voiced their options, the entire plan was approved. Therefore, a small group of dedicated people should make all the decisions during the construction phase.

First, I would select a panel of 5 men approved by the total church body, which would have the authority to make all the final decisions concerning the building project. I had learned from the experience that there was no way that the body members could build this new church building.

Before choosing the committee members, I knew who the five people would be and brought up this motion before the church. A motion was presented to the church body in a special called business meeting. Announced several weeks in advance so all members past, present who had in interest could come and express their opinions.

Crucial decisions that affect the total church body should not be secret, where only a few decide that affects everyone in the Church. A vote of 20 to sell the Church and three against selling in an unannounced motion in regular schedule business meetings was destined to have caused division in the Flock. This is what happened in 2013 in the First Baptist Church of Immokalee, and this is the reason why my wife's sister Karen had called my wife that night in March of 2013.

It was and is very important to get everyone involved in crucial decisions for the church. The flock's whole family needs to be involved in these decisions to keep harmony between the congregation and shepherd. We had learned this lesson in the 1980s.

It is only common sense to understand that many church people love their church and have opinions and concerns. Even those who had fallen out of fellowship should have the right to voice their opinion (they are still part of the Church family (the Flock). Maybe some consideration should be given even if some members did not live in Immokalee. All members should be notified of a crucial decision like selling the Promised Land. Then, in the 1980s, a vast project that would affect every member could voice their opinion before beginning.

The reason behind this thought was that members had supported the church for many years in the past. They had a right to speak and share their opinion. Even if we disagreed with their statement, no one would or should get angry with them. No one was excluded when we voted to build the new facility, unlike the decision to sell the new church facility in 2013.

When we took the vote in the 1980s to build, we wanted everyone to support this project or at least have a chance to voice their opinion without being demonized or removed from the church roles. It does not make common sense to begin a project starting with division, rumors, turmoil, backbiting before we got started. It would have been better to delay than start with this kind of division in our Flock.

Comparing the two decisions first, the decision to start the building program in 1983-1984, all the members were contracted, active, and those who were not. All church members were contacted, including those for starting the building project and those who were not sure about starting a building project.

Steve Price was my Aaron when we were considering building the Church and during the building process:

Steve Price, my interpreter, my Arron clearly explained the process and cleaned up the details. As Mosses had Aaron, his brother, I had Steve Price, my Christian brother who believed in me and that it was God's will that we build the new Church building.

> *Exodus 4: V10-14 And Moses said unto the LORD O my Lord, I am not eloquent, neither heretofore nor since thou has spoken unto thy servant: but I am slow of speech, and of a slow tongue V:14 Is not Aaron, the Levite, thy brother? I know that he can speak well. And also, behold he cometh forth to meet thee; and when he seeth thee, he will be glad in his heart.*

Of course, I am not comparing Steve or myself to Aaron or Mosses. But Mosses was slow of speech. The Lord understood that and gave him Aaron to speak for him. I am not a good public speaker. When I tried to use the excuse as Mosses did that I could not speak in public well, the Lord pressed the story of Aaron and Mosses upon my heart. I finally trusted my Lord, and he improved my ability to communicate and be the leader he wanted me to be.

I always have been. I seem blessed with the gift to write but cannot spell a lick or use proper grammar. I always have been that way. My grammar and spelling are horrible. But I have always felt if I could communicate my message, that is all that matters. You have been successful as long as someone gets the point and understands your message. As I tried to present things/ideas/updates, to be church body, Steve Price was always there to better explain/moderate what I was trying to communicate and make it clear, understandable, and reasonable. The Lord used him in a significant way keeping everyone confident and calm.

Also, an essential fact of this story is that we had minimal funds on hand to start the building process. We set out on faith that God would provide what was needed. The Church did have a new building fund, but there was not much money in it. But I, Brother Larry, the Deacons of 7 or 8, and those on the construction committee were assured by Steve; we would have the funds needed to complete the project.

**The "Miracle" of securing a construction loan:
Steve Price secured the construction loan for the
new building:**

Steve Price was in my Sunday school class, and we respected each other very much. Studying the word together, God had created a mysterious special relationship between Christian Brothers who love the Lord and believe in his Holly Word. If I know anything to be accurate, in this true story, if Steve Price had not been willing to be on the construction committee and had not gotten a commitment from the Bank for a construction loan, the new church building could not have been completed.

I do not believe that any other bank would have considered this project. Remember, I was a building contractor. I had lots of experience in securing construction loans. I do know what I am talking about. Other banks would have been thinking, "Let 250 Baptists build their church. Are you crazy? They can never agree on anything! They could never build a new Church building together." Most others, if not all, other banks would have turned down our construction loan.

Steve Price is a true friend: His faith is genuine, steadfast, even though he goes throw many tails in his life. Unlike me, who became bitter and blamed God for what happened to me for many years.

I have always considered Steve Price to be one of my Best Friends. He is a true friend that I could depend upon, day or night, good or bad. He was always there for me. I know that I have failed him in many ways for many years. But, he has also gone through some challenging personal issues, financial difficulties, just as I have.

I only mention this because of his witness and strength, and his continued faith in terrible times greatly influenced me. I had failed my Lord and was mad at him for about 20 years. Yet my Aaron/Peter, Steve Price, continued in his faith and grew closer to his Lord, going through worse circumstances than I had gone through. His confidence has always been a witness to me.

Romans 5:28 All things work for good for those who love the Lord.

God again needed Steve to take a stand in 2013. He helped lead the movement to save the Promised Land from being destroyed. I do not believe it was by accident that God called both Steve and me to stop the Promised Land from being sold. We were also the primary leaders in the Promised Land building.

Steve and I had similar situations where we lost most of our material wealth. But there was one big difference; Steve stayed in the Church. He accepted his crisis, where I blamed God and left him for a while. Yet, the Lord still used us both because even though I had failed my trials, my Lord always loved me even though I did not deserve it.

He was always there for me, in spirit, when I went through very similar situations. Please forgive me, Steve, for not being there for you when you needed me. I was still blaming God for my business failing issues and could not bring myself to go back to Immokalee. Like Job, Steve went a different path and even got closer to his Lord.

I did not. I rebelled and blamed God for my problems, murmured like the Children of Israel, and wondered why he had not protected me from the issues of life in business. Steve was faithful. I was not. Read the story about Job in the Bible, and this will give you more insight into the struggles in life and two different approaches to dealing with those issues.

It is a mystery, but I have always felt very close to Steve because we never spent much time together. We fished together a few times but were never buddy/ buddy. Instead, there seemed to be an extraordinary spiritual relationship/ bond that the Lord had set in motion through many personal and business experiences that we had together over many years. I knew of Steve when I was a teacher in High School at Immokalee High. But, unfortunately, he was not in the classes I taught.

With Steve in Control, the Funds for the building were always there when we needed them:

If you know anything about building, you have to have the funds ready when you need them. You could not stop and start the construction.

With Steve, the funds were always there. As a result, we moved forward rapidly in the construction phase, finishing the vast project in record time. He was the most important person on the Construction committee and gave his time, personal donations, support, and life, for this two-year project.

I know that Steve would not want me to write about these facts, but I believe it is essential that the First Baptist church members understand his role in its Journey to the Promised Land.

May God continue to bless Steve Price for him, letting the Lord use him in the manner he did in the past and present.

Steve Price sells the old church property, and the "Promised Land" is now debt-free: another "Miracle" we move into a debt-free new faultily.

By the way, one of our goals of the construction committee with minimal funds was not only to build the Church but to complete it debt-free. The actions of Steve Price are the main reason we reached this goal. Not only did we build the church for pennies compared to the cost of standard construction, but Steve, with the Lord's help, by himself, sold the old church property after we had vacated it. As a result, we paid off the debt on the brand new building. We have **paid off in Full** because Steve Price let the Lord use him during that period.

Steve will get his reward at the judgment seat of Christ:

Steve never will and never has asked for any glory or appreciation for his work, but he sure desires it. But his steadfastness and his faith and attitude at that time continue to bless me and renew my faith.

The Lord will reward him when he gets to heaven. Steve will have a massive mansion in heaven, walk-on Gold's streets, and get a well done though Good and Faithfull servant. But, unfortunately, my rewards may be burned up. I was faulted and was missing in action for about 20 years.

2 Timothy 4 V. 7-8, I have fought a good fight, I have finished my course, I kept the faith; V 8. Henceforth there is laid up for me a crown of righteousness, which the Lord, the righteous judge3, shall give me on that day, not only to me but also to all who love his appearing.

I know that Steve Price continues to fight the good fight at the First Baptist Church in Immokalee until he believes he has done all he can do, and the Lord leads him elsewhere. May God continue to pour out his Holy Spirit and be with Steve Price, which I know that he will.

Sam Lee and the deacon's role in the Building of the church facility:

I believe the Lord always has in his Church body members that he needs to get the job done. All we have to do is let the Lord lead us to them.

There was another person whom I have not mentioned yet in this true story, Sam Lee, a Deacon Brother. God placed him not on the construction committee because his talents/gifts were unnecessary. That was just the nuts and bolts of the building process. But Sam has the advantage of taking the most complicated issue, which we might talk about for hours, breaking it down into a simple statement in minutes, and communicating this to the church and deacon body, especially in construction meetings. I believe that this is superintelligence that few people have as a gift from God.

God be praised; we had a great group of Deacons while building the church. They were supportive while we were considering the new building plans and during its construction. If the church or pastor believes it will build a new building without a strong deacon body, they are sadly mistaken. I believe any pastor who thinks he can do it independently is very severely mistaken and out of the Lord's will. A vast construction project takes up too much of your time. If a pastor takes total control, his spiritual responsibilities will be neglected.

At that time, our leader, Brother Larry Finley, sought out a deacon body to do what the scriptures set in place for them to do. At the same time, I was getting the church construction started, and while Larry studied the word, he and the other deacons ministered to the body of the church.

If a Church Leader does not choose to have several Deacons to help him, there is probably something wrong with that leader. He may want to be a dictator and not a Sheppard. I believe that my Lord has provided the necessary men in every church body to become deacons. They must be sought out. God has provided all the different gifts/talents in every Church body needed to carry that Church forward. **Romans: Chapter 12** points out these facts. The entire chapter should be read to get an understanding of its meaning. I believe this verse also includes the body of Christ in his church.

Different gifts have been given by God's grace. Each person should honestly search their heart and mind to determine which gift or gifts they have. If we do not use these God-given talents, we may lose them. Respect is earned by self-examination to ensure that you do not use skills you do not possess. Some may have more gifts than one. The story of the talents also applies here *to Mathew 25: V, 14-30 that we must use the skills/gifts.*

> *Romans 12: V 3, For I say, through the grace given unto me, to every man that is among you, not to think of himself more highly than he ought to thinks, but to think soberly, according as God hath dealt to every man the measure of faith. V:4 For as we have many members in one body, and all members have not the same office. V. 5, So we being many are one body in Christ, and every one members one of another. V6. Having then gifts differing according to the grace that is give to us, whether prophecy, let us prophesy, according to the proportion of faith. V7. Ministry, let us wait on the ministering, or he that teacheth on teaching. V8. Or he the exhorteth on exhortation: he that giveth, let him do it with liberality he that ruleth, with diligence, he that shows mercy, with cheerfulness.*

I believe these verses teach us that in every body of Christ, the church, by God's grace, both men and <u>women,</u> have been given the gifts or talents needed in the body to function. The problem arises when some try to do things they do not have the skills or talents. The whole church needs to recognize and place faith in those it believes have the gifts and talents given by God's grace to individual members. Only by self-examination can we determine if we have specific skills. Many of us think more of ourselves than we ought. The Church needs all the gifts of its members to make the church function. Every gift/talent is important. Some members have the talent to teach, others to witness, and others to comfort the sick. One talent is not more important than another. The important thing is to use the gift/talent that God has given you. We need to be careful not to develop too much pride. Some have business knowledge, management skills; others do not. Some are more spiritual than others. God has put all the church members to form one body so his church can function and grow.

In the past, when we were considering building the new church building on the "Promised Land," it seemed as if many recognized their gifts/talents that God gave them and used them for his glory.

Our church business was managed by committees that reported to the church monthly for the most part. The pastor was involved in everything but controlled nothing. His primary role was to be the pastor and study the word. He was there for spiritual leadership.

Romans: 12: 9-16 has a lot more to say about the relationship of those in the Church body.

> *V. 9. Let love be without hypocrisy, abhor that which is evil, cling to that which is good. V 10 Be the kindly affectionate one to the another with brotherly love in honor and preferring one another. V. 11 Not slothful in business, fervent in spirit, serving the Lord. V. 12 Rejoicing in hope; patient in tribulations; continuing diligently in prayer.*

Jesus taught us by example, by washing the disciples' feet, that the Leader/Preacher was to be a servant and a leader at the same time. **Lead with Compassion;** I defined it...

> *John 13: V. 13 Ye call me Master and Lord and ye say well: for so I am. V. 14 If I then your Lord and Master, have washed your feet, ye also ought to wash one another's feet. V 15. For I have given you an example that ye should do as I have done to you. V 16. Verliy, verily, I say onto you. The servant is not greater than his Lord, neither he that is sent greater than he that sent him.*

When the Lord told me to write this true story and history, I did not realize he would lead me into many different side streets. I make no apology for taking these side streets. But, again, I am letting the Spirit of my Lord guide me in this story. The more I put on paper, the more he leads me. I am amazed because the Lord, with his tender mercies, continues to speak to my heart, mind, and soul.

> *First Corinthians: 1:V. 27: But God hath chosen the foolish things of the world to confound the wise, and God hath chosen the weak things of the world to confound the things which are mighty> V. 28 And base things of the world, and things chosen, yea, and things which are not, to bring to nothing things that are. V. 29: That no flesh should glory in his presence.*

During perpetration and planning for the New Church building, all Deacons were supportive and had a big part in the project. All these men had unique talents that the Lord had put into the Church body at precisely the right time. None of us were perfect, far from it, but we all believed, were willing to be used, had faith, and did take a stand for our Lord.

We put feet into our prayers and did things for our Lord. We did not just sit back and pray. We put feet into our prayers. We did as the book of James says:

> *James 1:22 But be ye doers of the word and not hearers only, deceiving your own selves. James 2:17 Even so faith, if it hath not works is dead, being alone.*

Jimmy Lanier, Bud Shelly, Bill **Bethea**, Robert Rice, John Gibbons, Morris Lewis, Jimmy Lanier, Havel Chandler, Sam Lee, and Gray Bates are exceptional men. Our Lord used in a significant time in the history of the First Baptist Church. All these men were appointed deacons during Brother Larry Finley's ministry at the First Baptist Church. All had an essential part in the Journey to the Promised Land and the building process and used their God-given talents to complete the facility. So again, I believe that God has the right members of the body (the church in this case) at the right time to get the task done that he wants to get done. All we have to do is to listen and trust him in faith. All these great men had faith and let God use them.

Also, I cannot remember any fundamental disagreement in the membership in the 1980s about the proposal to build the facility ourselves after we met with Bobby Jones. Yes, there were many questions, and we took the time to discuss them and answer them. But we all became of one mind. Those who doubted either changed their mind or decided not to voice their options anymore. We were all of one mindset. We believed it was God's will that we move to the Promised Land and build a new facility in the center of Immokalee for the Glory of God.

Steve Price has a backbone like John the Baptist:

Steve Price always had the spine to take a stand when it was not popular. But he always did it with respect, under-standing, and compassion. I have to respect that. I have also been in this situation when no one else, but me and the Lord, believed what was right, and it is tough to stand alone when that event occurs.

> *Matthew 3:V 7 But when he saw many of the Pharisees and Saducees come to his baptism, he said unto them, O generation of vipers, who hath warned you to flee from the wrath to Come Luke 3: 19 But Herod, the trarch, being reproved by John the Baptist for all the evils which Herod had done.*

But any one person and the Lord is a majority. Therefore, Satan will attack that person more than anyone else. Satin did it in my personal life and Steve Price's past and present. I am waiting for Satan to attack and break out his fiery darts against me for writing this book. This may have been one reason why it took so long for me to write this story. I was afraid of Satan's attacks. I was worried and did not want to go through all the battles Satan (Fiery Darts) would bring against me, which I know are headed toward me now.

But sometimes, things happen when you have to take a stand or die. I was at that point with the things happening on April 14, 2013, in the church service at First Baptist Church in Immokalee. I am writing this story a fast as possible since I fear the worst for my Christian brothers and those who have put so much effort, money, sacrifice, blood, sweat, and tears into the Church's building. They gave so much to the new facility to enable the Church body to grow and lead 1000s to Jesus our Lord.

Don't let Satan deceive you, Brothers, in 2013:

Some say that the Church building is too large for the modern world and that not many people go to Church today.

> *Mark 13 5:V 5-6 And Jesus answering them, began to say, Take heed lest any man deceives you: V:6 For many shall come in my name, saying I am the Christ, and shall deceive many.*

There are plenty of Churches overflowing with people led by the right Shepard and a positive direction with a loving spirit. I visited one of these was full even if it is not Easter Sunday and has three services every Sunday to reach many people who want to visit that church. This Church atmosphere is positive, loving, caring, goal setting, witnessing, and exciting. There is more of a need today than ever for a Church that shows companionship and love in 2013. The world of 2020 is a challenging Christian time in history. The Lord returning cannot be far off. The youth of 2020 have been indoctrinated by school systems that have abounded Christian teaching and American history. Many times they teach the opposite of God's Word.

> *First Corinthians 15: V 51. Behold, I show you a mystery: We shall not all sleep, but we shall all be changed, V52. In a moment, in the twinkling of an eye, at the last trump, for the trumpet, shall sound and the dead shall be raised, incorruptible, and we shall be changed. V 53. For this, corruptible must put on in corruption, and this mortal must put on immortality.*

This event is very close, I believe. Feed the sheep with meat from the word, no longer milk, watered-down, but MUST BE WITH COMPASSION AND LOVE. That Church will fill up fast. People today have so many problems and issues to deal with and do not know where to turn. Satan knows that his time is short, and he is doing everything possible to make the life of a Christian complex full of trials and tribulations.

Construction Committee Members:

The Construction committee members were Steve Price, John Giddens, Robert Rice, Jack Queen, and Morris Lewis. Steve, my legal and financial moderator, did all the accounting and billing. For steadfastness/compassion, Jack Queen donated all fill dirt, tree removal, land clearing on the property, parking lots, and paving. John Gideon and Robert Rice were steadfast workers to complete the task and input from the Church, go-betweens. Morris building plans for the church, leadership, direction, construction experience, and supervising the construction.

When we started the building, I knew that we did not need the general Contractor except to pull the building permit. Bother Bobby Jones was a lot of help. I did understand Brother Bobby would not have the time to spend on the job every day, and we agreed that I would be there for him. Morris Lewis had to be on the grounds almost every day from the start to finish this massive building project. Brother Bobby was a big help in locating suppliers and others since he had just built almost the same building. He had great insight into where it was best to buy specific materials necessary to build the Church. He gave me good advice and information to make the best decisions in the building process.

Brother Larry has unique dedication service at the property before construction begins:

Brother Larry had a dedication and prayer service on the grounds before construction. He also had a tent revival on the property. Revivals in those days and today are significant to the Church and the pastor. Revivals regenerate the Churches spirit. A church that does not have revivals is missing a special gift from God.

Romans 12: V1-2. I beseech you therefore, brethren, by the mercies of God, that ye present your bodies a living sacrifice, holy, acceptable unto God, which is your reasonable service. V.2. And be not conformed to this world, but be ye transformed, by the renewing of your mind, that ye may prove what is that good and acceptable, and perfect will of God.

Renewing your mind is more than only reading the Bible and studying the word. I also believe it means remembering your past personal history, Christian experience and renewing your spirit through revivals. So what better way to rekindle your spirit than an old fashion Church revival where the word of God is preached in boldness and truth?

I believe Brother Larry doubts my commitment to the project?

In the last part of July and especially in Aug., Brother Larry phoned me many times, asking when I was coming home to manage the project. I told him very calmly and clearly that I was in constant contact with those who knew want needed to be complete. I told Brother Larry that I needed this time to be with my family because I recognized the long road ahead, and this was a two-year project, not just a month.

Satan never gave up trying to destroy a building on the Promise Land

We are finally ready to start the building process. The Permits are pulled, but <u>WAIT</u>! **Satan** attacks us again. Our pastor and the spiritual leader told us that God called him to the First Baptist Church to build a new church on the Promised Land, <u>resigned suddenly</u>. It was a rapid and surprising event for us all. Within days a few days after his resignation, he left the Church and Immokalee.

Everything was ready to begin. At that time, I usually spent the summer months in the Fl. Keys, fishing, building homes, and working on a rental business there. It was our family time for many years since I was so busy working hundreds of hours. I had very little family time during the farming and harvest time in Immokalee. I worked in the construction business, Grocery business, rental business, and hardware business.

Later as I reflect on the total picture, I also believe this event was in God's overall plan, although I did not like it. But when it happened, it was an incredible experience to the Church, which could have shaken our faith. I believe it was a miracle that we did not abandon the building project at that time.

Satan's fiery darts continue to try to destroy the Promised Land: Not only has Brother Larry resigned as a pastor, but now we did not have any fill dirt for foundation because the county will not give Jack Queen digging permits:

I am not sure which happen first. But the fiery darts of Satan begin to be tossed to stop the church building project on the "Promised Land." To <u>My Shock</u> and great surprise Brother,

Larry resigned, as a pastor, while I was in the Keys, and then within a few days, Jack Queen found out that he could not get the county's permit to dig the dirt needed for the church building foundation. So there was some type of delay in issuing it, Satan's delay in my mind.

For many years since that, I had always thought Brother Larry had lost his faith again and had abounded me the second time as he did at the old church construction meeting when I resigned led by God from the first construction committee. But, unfortunately, Brother Larry left the church before I returned to Immokalee from the Keys. I do not know why he left.

Now here we are, no dirt for the foundation and no pastor for the Church. The leader who told us he was sent to Immokalee to build on the Promised Land had abandoned us. A great start towards the construction of the new Church Building, right? I did not leave the Keys. I stayed my usual time in Aug. about 15th. I never saw Brother Larry during the construction. Not until a homecoming event many years later, 2011 Church Home Coming,

Brother Larry is now gone. Our Church was starting a major construction project. Will the Promised Land survive?

Four others and I now had complete authority, given by the church in a special business meeting that all members, past and present, were notified about to continue the project, but should we? With our leader gone! <u>To my memory, the church body, the Flock, remained calm and was not concerned about the construction project, which to me was **another MIRACLE**</u>.

Therefore, we stayed on track for the beginning of the construction project. But the church body could have easily said we cannot continue this project. Without a pastor to support the old church, we may not have the income to continue a new construction project. If any of this happened, I was not aware of it, but remember, we had a solid Deacon base to answer all questions and quite the storm. This was **Another MIRACLE**.

None were perfect, but all had faith and were willing to be used, put themselves on the front line, move forward, and do something.

An interim pastor is now on the scene: Pastor Colvard

The next event was the interim pastor. Who would this be? How much influence would he put on the construction committee? Would he support the building effort? Many other questions, and concerns, came to my mind.

I believe this was **another MIRACLE** in God's overall plan. The interim pastor did just what he was supposed to do, in my mind, and trusted the foundation already set before he got there and left the construction committee alone. I cannot remember him even making any suggestions to the construction committee. We met at least once a week at the First Bank of Immokalee conference room; Steve Price provided this meeting area, private and convenient.

The "Miracle" of God providing the fill dirt:

I did not panic. I believed the Lord would give us a way to continue. My faith was solid as a rock. My Lord had given me the experiences/test earlier in my walk with him to move forward in faith. I was now committed to the building project. I had the faith that my Lord wanted us to build on his Promised land. I had experiences with the ups and downs of a construction project. The Lord had me prepared for the battle. **I knew we were doing the Lord's will**.

> *Matthew 6: V8: Be not ye, therefore, like unto them; for your, Father knoweth what things ye need of before ye ask him.*

Within a few days, Deacon Jimmy Lanier contacted me and said that the company he worked for, Collier Company, a few miles down the road, was put in an orange grove and needed a place to put a landfill. Now again, say, can you honestly believe this by accident? I know this was **another of the many MIRACLES** that the Lord provided. Jack Queen got with Jimmy, he said he had the dump trucks, and we still got the fill needed for the foundation, for free and on time to keep our schedule. It was a very big-ticket item in our construction budget.

Better yet, even for Jack Queen, who did not even have to dig up the fill, which cut his expenses. He only had to pick it up, similar to what happened many years ago when Jack Queen moved the fill dirt to the pound area at the west end of the "Promised Land." Earlier in this book, Collier Company donated the fill dirt for the pound area under Brother Babb's ministry. Jack Queen was the contractor who moved the fill-in both incidents over 20 years apart. It was almost the same story that Brother Babb had shared with me, which happened when he ministered to the Church. Do you believe this was an accident? Those who have ears let them hear. O Ye of little faith. The past experiences keep repeating themselves for the future.

I wonder how Jack Queen would have voted in the decision to sell the Church. He had passed away. I believe he would have voted not to sell.

Jack Queen Begins removing the trees and Brings in the fill dirt:

I constantly communicated with Jack Queen, a construction committee member who was the expert in doing what he did for a living, who had started removing the trees in the building's footprint and parking lot area. We had worked on many building projects together in the past. This footprint, Bobby Jones, the contractor, whom I can't even remember his name, and I had put down stakes where the church building foundation would be. We set the grade stakes together for the fill. We also marked the trees that needed to be cut down inside the foundation.

Jack Queen continues to remove trees:

Most of these trees had been there for over 75 years, probably longer, since Robert's had set aside the property for the new church in the future. Jack's equipment spent countless hours working. Yet, he never sent a bill for the work to my knowledge. Even on that day, easily $25-$30,000, if contracted out. Jack Queen did a lot of work for the Church, which he did not bill us. Remember, we never asked Jack Queen to donate. He did it because he loved his Lord and the Lord led him to do so. Maybe he did charge for fuel only, but you would have to ask Steve Price if Jack ever sent a tree removal bill.

Jack had also committed to providing all the fill dirt needed for the project as a donation, as I recall. The cost of that would have been close to $50,000.00. Remember, I was a contractor and understood the costs of construction.

Jack Queen was a Quiet, Godly man who showed his love through his actions.

Jack Queen has gone to be with his Lord. Jack Queen was a doer. He was quiet in his leadership and his giving. I am sure that our father has welcomed him into heaven and said, "Well done, thou good and faithful servant. His wife Marylyn is still alive at the first writing of this book in 2013. I hope that the deacon and other brothers and sisters in Christ visit her and console her. Her husband had a big quiet role in the Journey to the "Promised Land." I am fearful that deacons often forget that they are called spiritual leaders and not just business leaders in the Church.

I believe Romans chapter 12 points this out. Unfortunately, many churches get into trouble when the deacons believe their calling is to manage the Church's business. But spiritual gifts and management gifts are two different types of skills. True, you may have more than one gift, and you are responsible for using all the gifts God has given you. But I fear that sometimes when a person becomes a deacon, they lose sight of their spiritual responsibilities, which are much more complex than the business management responsibilities of running a church.

I hope that the First Baptist Church's deacons have remembered their spiritual responsibilities of caring for the needy and the widows. Acts 6: 1-8 explicitly gives this task to the deacons. Mrs. Marylyn Queen is one widow that should be honored and cared for and visited often. Her husband deserves that from the church, and other widows also should be visited. But Jack Queen did a lot to make the "Promised Land" possible. She should be remembered, respected, and honored for her husband's sake.

Brother Larry left the church in 1986 and never preached in the new building until 2011. Home Coming:

On the phone, I remember asking Brother Larry, before he left, why he was going just when the construction was beginning. He said the Lord told him it was time for him to leave. He told me that the task God gave him to do in Immokalee was completed, and it was time for him to move elsewhere. I doubted his words for many years. I still often wonder what the real reason he left when he did was.

But, again, my brother in Christ, Steve Price, a great foundation building block and cornerstone, another Peter Jesus' disciple of the First Baptist Church in Immokalee, gave me comfort, confidence and we kept moving forward. But it was not easy to control my questions Christians are their own worst enemies; most do not let the Lord or trust him to take care of life issues, including myself. You would think, I would have learned by now, to trust him, but the flesh is tough to control. So Paul stated, "I do what I know not to do. It is Sin within me".

Romans 7:V15-25, V15: For that which I do I understand not; for what I would that do I not; but what I hate that do I. V18 for I know (that in me this is I my flesh) dwelleth in me no good thing; for TO WILL is present with me, but how to perform that which is g

Even Paul battled with the flesh. He had to put on the whole armor of God to fight his flesh and sin.

Ephesians 6:11-17: V 11. Put on the whole armor of God, that ye may be able to stand against the wiles of the devil. V.12 For we wrestle not against flesh and blood, but against principalities, and against power, and against the rulers of the darkness of this world, against spiritual wickedness in high places. Wherefore, take unto you the whole armor God, that ye may be able to withstand in the evil day, and having done all that stand. V 16 Above all taking the shield of faith, with which ye shall be able to quench all the fiery darts of the wicked. V 17, And take the helmet of salvation, and the sword of eh Spirit, which is the Word of God.

I have often thought that those who accursed Brother Larry of just wanting to build a Church building his glory and pride thought about his leaving. The fact that Brother Larry decided to leave the First Baptist Church of Immokalee before the Church started construction should have made them believe they had misjudged his motives. To My knowledge Brother, Larry has never preached in the new facility until a home-coming service in 2011.

The importance of having a Church Home Coming Service:

I will bring up this side thought as the Lord speaks to me. Any person or leader who does not believe in having a Home-Coming service, which has been a tradition at First Baptist of Immokalee for years, is not thinking about the good of his flock. He may not have enough compassion for his sheep or for the hundreds of others who continue to believe that the First Baptist Church of Immokalee is their home Church. I know that my wife planned her October calendar that she would be able to attend the yearly Home Coming Service in Immokalee.

After all, that is what the Seminole word Immokalee means, MY HOME. It is a great event when the older ones enlighten the younger ones of the history, speaking in wisdom since they have already experienced the trials of life that our Church and Nation faces. I believe this is a reminder of where the

Church foundation came from. Therefore, I would strongly suggest that the Flock bring a motion to have a Church Home Coming as part of Church policy every October, beginning the new church year. This would secure this wonderful worship and fellowship forever and make it binding on whoever was in the pulpit. This event is not for the Shepard but the spiritual well-being of the flock.

Now let me get back on track and continue this true and critical story.

The building construction continues: I believe everything written about in the Long Journey had to happen before we could get to this point in the facility construction phase. So this is the Journey of "Miracles" that finally got us to the Promised Land.

We continued to construct the church. It took more and more of my time away from my business responsibilities. I had a business partner during this time. He agreed to sell all the materials, from our B & L hardware store to the Church, at our cost. He did not seem to care that I was spending a lot of time working on the Church building project. Not long after the Church Construction was completed, although we had been close friends from our High School days until now, our partnership was over, and our friendship seemed to be damaged. I have no bad feelings or judgment here and only mention it because, at that time, it was very hurtful and stressful. But, again, Steve

Price, my Friend, was there to help, advise and comfort me through the ordeal. I believe it was good much later in life, and everything would work out for me. Romans 8: 28 All things work together for good to them that love God,... I can now understand the Lord's intervention in this troubling time through hindsight.

A Christian man Jake Blackburn made it possible for me to have the time to work on the Church building project. "MIRACLE"

Jake and Doris Blackburn were two of the best people and Christians I have ever known. God has taken them to be with him now. I believe God sent Jake to help me run B & L Grocery to have time to devote to the Church building project and other spiritual things the Lord had used me for at the Church.

I have never witnessed any more vital Christian witness than Doris, who was sick for many years, confined to a chair, and in terrible pain, yet kept her faith, and she always had a positive attitude about life and my Lord. I would have been one of those who blamed God and would not have kept the faith and finished the race. I thanked God for her witness many times, thinking about her witness often. My wife and I visited her several time during her illness. She was a great witness for my Lord and never lost her faith.

The significant part of this story is my belief that God had years ago planned this event to happen. It is a continued theme throughout this book. The Lord is in control. We need to use our <u>hindsight to straighten our faith and insight into how God works in our lives</u>.

When I was a very young boy, I worked for Billy Crisp at ShopWorth as a bag boy and work stock. Billy had hired Jake Blackburn to manage the Grocery store after I started working there. I was in high school and on my own. It is how I made my living at that time. I learned a lot from Billy Crisp and Jake. Both were and acted as Christians in their daily lives.

Now we move forward for many years. Blocker & Lewis decided to get into the Grocery business. It is not a business I liked, but somehow I made the business profitable. Unfortunately, this Grocery store already had two significant disadvantages in becoming very profitable.

Since I was a deacon at that time and because of my convictions, the store could not open on Sunday, nor could the store sell beer or wine. Even if I had not been a deacon, I could not have done these things. The Church covenant forbids members to do these things. <u>I wonder how many Church members even get a copy of their Church Covenant and understand their responsibilities; when they become members of a Church</u>.

There are hundreds of hours per week involved in running a Grocery Store and very little time for anything else. I was committed to somehow turning a failing business when we purchased it to make it profitable. It took a total commitment to this business. I had little time to do anything else. One day Jake Blackburn, who loved the Grocery Store business, came by. He had been in the Grocery store business all his life. He came by out of nowhere and asked for a job **(ANOTHER MIRACLE)**. I did not seek him out. I believe God sent him to me. He enjoyed meeting the people and enjoyed being busy and working the very long hours required.

He had retired already and was not concerned about making money at this point in his life. He just wanted to be needed and wanted a job. He was already in his 70's when he came to work for us at B & L.

Therefore, Jake took over the day-to-day routines, and I still made the head management decisions. He loved it and did not mind the long hours. If God had not sent Jake Blackburn to help me, I would not have had the time to do many of the tasks my Lord had laid upon me.

One was the visitation program in the old church in the center of Immokalee. One year we had 125 people saved through that program while Brother Larry was the pastor in Immokalee. One of the many factors that started the church to consider we needed to build another larger Church.

This book was not written to give me any credit but to give my Lord all the praise he sent Jake to help me. He was the person I worked for when I was a young boy, and now he works for me. I believe any success that I had with my Lords' help and guidance, Jake Blackburn and Doris, will receive their rewards in Heaven. I believe this is a practical, real-life event that others may consider when deciding what talents/gifts

God has given them. Again, it points out a continued theme throughout this story of how God uses things and people to accomplish his goals.

It is similar to the woman who only had a mite to give, but that mite was greater than millions because she had given her all. No one should look down on anyone who uses the talents/ gifts, no matter how small, to our Lord. Our Lord can use their little gifts to make possible very great things happen. In life's journey, you hear about these types of stories all the time.

I believe that God had planned and foreknew this many years when he placed me in a situation working for Jake when I was a boy. If I did not have this experience with Jake, I might have missed God's Blessing of letting Jake work for me. Therefore, I might not have had the time to do the very few things that I believe the Lord leads me to do, giving him all the credit since I did not do anything without my Lord's help. I only let the Lord use my unworthy body, mind, and soul. In my strength, I did nothing.

The Decorating and other committee's role in building the new Church:

By now, the construction was moving forward at a rapid pace. Everything was moving very smoothly. It became time to select colors, carpet, seating, organs, sound systems, Kitchen equipment, gym flooring, family life center, trees and plants, and on and on. I remember thinking that this would be a good opportunity for other members to get involved. Therefore, I suggested setting up committees to cover these and many other items and details. Our Lord had provided all the different body members needed to make good decisions in many different areas of need in this building process.

> *Romans 12:V1-20, V3 …God hath dealt with every man the measure of faith. V4. We have many members in one body, and all members have not the same office. Through verse 20.*

Many of the flock were involved in the building project now. Peggy Bethea, Bennie, and Brunette Starling, Havel Chandler, to name a few, and others were on the many different committees. Bill Heart, phone, and P A systems did a lot of work on those systems. Havel Chandler chaired the sound equipment and musical equipment, and many others on those committees gathered ideas, suggestions, costs, and bids used in the Church's construction. I am sure God did bless them for their service in building his Church on the "Promised Land."

Sometimes too many making decisions isn't good:

Thank God we let them recommend, and the construction committee voted and gave the final approval of their recommendations. If not, we may have still been waiting for a final decision, just joking, but it was pretty intensive. But this fact reinforces my belief that you can have too many people in a democracy making decisions, and therefore nothing moves forward in an organized business manner. Sometimes, many choices must be completed, and things must keep moving due to time schedules. What is more important is that those involved in making the decisions have the gift/talents to do so and have the flock's proven faith and trust to lead the flock.

Some situations call for action and move forward rapidly. They are not just waiting for things to happen by chance. Goals and direction should always have time limits to reach these goals. Sometimes it is best to have a few who are willing to put in the top priority of their life the welfare of the Church and commit to that with prayer and dedication.

Anyway, we muddle through that construction phase and put all the many different parts together. Too many making decisions is not an excellent way to manage any project. It confuses. Some have to be followers. Yes, all should have input, but there must be some trust in the leadership.

Any Christian, I believe, should be able to determine if their leadership is deceiving them. I have had this experience in my journey through life when a Christian brother would tell me something, and the Lord would speak to my heart that tells me the statement was not valid. After investigating the information, I still heard a small voice saying that the information was not accurate. By their works are the known. This is what the Bible teaches.

> *James 1.V 8 If any man among you seem to be religious, and bridleth not his tongue, but decieveth his own heart, this man's religion is in van. Mathew 23. V. 28 Even so ye also outwardly appear righteous unto men, but within ye are full*

of hypocrisy and iniquity. Mathew 24. V 4. Take heed that no man deceive you.

We continued to build day after day. Bobby Jones was spending a lot less time on the project than I had hoped. He was hired to be the project manager, but it took more and more of my time. He knew that I was there to fill in the times he had to be gone.

A lot of the work, the churchmen, stepped up and did. They did I the framing of all the classrooms and the shingles on the roof. Almost every week, we had a project for someone to do. Some members did clean up, which was also an essential task. There was plenty of work and options for anyone who wanted to get involved with the project. It was a happy time. Everyone was busy doing something.

We saved thousands and thousands, and donations were pouring into the Church building funds. Steve Price managed this. He did all the bookwork. Steve Price wrote out all the checks for the work, subcontractors, and supplies and materials, which took two committee members to sign. He kept a computerized type sheet of the bills and funds available to be spent. He and I gave weekly reports of the progress to the Church body every Wednesday night. This practice stopped many rumors that always seem to be present. Remember, we did not have all the funds necessary to complete this project, and the First Bank of Immokalee at because of Steve Price's leadership, loaned the First Baptist church the funds to construct the building.

Bennie Zipperer did the entire sprinkler system for the new Church. The sprinkler system must be completed before getting the certificate of occupancy, the C. O.

We were finally coming to the end of the project of the Sanctuary. The family life center was on track. It was time to consider the sprinkler system for the grounds. We appointed Bennie Zipperer, who had the experience working for the water company to design the system, and he volunteered his labor to do most of the work.

But wait, another fiery dart from Satan was tossed at us. Remember, without the sprinkler system completed, and we could not get the C. O. because we could not complete the land scraping or lay the sod.

The first part of this project was to put in a well. Bennie knew how to put a shallow well that did not require a permit at that time. However, the well failed and would not supply the amount of water needed for the entire project. Therefore, he had to apply for a deep well permit from the county. This story is similar to three different times county permits were needed.

Bennie goes to the county officials and tells him that he cannot get well for several months. It would mean that the total building project would be delayed for months. Bennie talks to everyone he can think of in the county to get a permit. He finally talks to a person who gives him the advice to speak to one of the county commissars that he may know. Bennie knew Jack Price, no relationship to Steve Price. Therefore,

Bennie talked with Jack Price at that time, and Jack approved the permit. **MIRACLE!.**

We purchased the material, and I believe Bennie Zipperer did most of the physical labor with a few other church members helping him. I think Floyd Crews and Murray helped him. Other members loan him the digging equipment to dig the trenches needed to install the pipe for the sprinkler system. Bennie also spent many hours framing work and roofing, and other projects required to construct the building.

I also remember Robert Rice and John Gideon helping in the area, trees and plants, and many other things. Everyone helped where and when they could.

I had known Bennie and Linda Zipperer since their high school days when they were in my class when I was a teacher at Immokalee High School. Unfortunately, Linda, his wife, has passed in 2019, but Bennie and I still fish together in 2020, often, and are still very close friends. Linda, his wife, I hired her just out of high school to become my private secretary for over 20 years when I managed B and L Hardware.

Bennie Zipperer was one of those members (the remnant) who also believed in the Promised Land and was a close friend of Brother Babb Adams. He has shared with me many facts, which I did not know at the time, of how he had talked with Brother Babb about selling the Promised Land—later finding out that Brother Babb had told us both the same things about the sale of the Church.

Bennie Zipperer also continued to use his many talents for many years (probably 40) kept up the Churches maintenance until he decided to move to the Fl. Keys in 2017.

Melvin Taylor does the Trim work for the entire Church: Bessie Taylors' son mentioned earlier in this book.

Melvin Taylor worked for me for years in my construction business. I believe he was the best trim carpenter in the industry. He was the son of Bessie Taylor. Remember, Bessie Taylor was the person I lived with during my high school days. So God used this boyhood experience to meet Melvin while I stayed with Bessie Taylor, written about earlier in the book. He hung most of the doors and trimmed them throughout.

This is a picture of Melvin's woodwork enclosing the baptistery area with swinging doors and a wooden cross behind the pulpit.

the entire project. But his finest work was the doors he built from my design in the Baptistery, behind the pulpit.

He installed, with help, of course, the large wood poles/planks in the rocked area behind the pulpit. They were supposed to have been crosses, but the decorating committee felt that would be too many crosses. I disagreed with their decision. I suggested it was the right thing to do but dropped it after it became an issue. I still believe that the poles/planks should have been crosse. I hope that these poles/planks in the back of the pulpit will be made into crosses as per the original design one day. It would be simple to do.

We also had a similar issue with the crosses in both foyers. The committee did not want them there either. I did not understand why, and this time used my authority and put them in the rocks anyway. I do not believe you can have too many crosses. If it were not for the cross, there would be no need for a Church. We need to continue to see the cross to help us remember what God did for us before, the foundation of the world.

This picture was taken in 2020 of Inside the Church, the Rock wall that Carol Ford completed, and wood beams that Melvin Taylor installed. The original sanctuary had wooden pews inside of chairs, which would seat 250 people. Also, the actual carpet color was blood red which represented the blood of Jesus, which he shed for us on the cross.

The rocks behind the pulpit and in the foyer:

The rocked area behind the pulpit and the Foyer were ideas I got from my personal building experience. This is because of my experience building my own home on Lemon Tree Dr.; This is an essential side street that has to be part of this true story since I believe; my Lord even used this experience to prepare me for the future.

It is a long true story about the building of my home in Immokalee, but I know I had a bearing and paved the way for an essential **MIRACLE** accrued in the Church Foyer many years later. Please keep this in mind as I continue this true story. Every time I think about this, it brings tears to my eyes and joy to my heart. Not the building of my home that is not important. But how God used that experience also to prepare me for the construction of his church many years later.

The Lord used the construction of my dream home to prepare me for the future construction of his Church.

My business partner and I had an opportunity to purchase 40 ac., near Lake Trafford. We were a close family, and we decided to make it a family complex. Therefore, we divided the property into 10 ac. Plots and drew straws to determine which part of the property we would get. I only wanted one particular piece, and this is the one that I drew.

We all had homes we needed to sell before building our new dream homes. At that time, I was running a hardware store and construction business. Brother Babb, many years ago, had asked me to teach Sunday School. I can remember many times that I turned the the building of homes in Immokalee over to the Lord to watch over the process, while I studied the Bible getting ready for my Sunday School Class, in the office of B and L Hardware. Crews were pouring tie beams, installing roofs, etc., which I had complete confidence in when I usually would have been on-site.

However, when I finally decided to teach Sunday School, I asked the Lord and suggested taking care of these projects while studying. Of course, I understand that you are not supposed to bargain with your heavenly father. But I still talked to him like a good earthly father.

Matthew 7:V. 7-11 If ye then being evil, know how to give good gifts unto your children, how much more shall your Father, who is in heaven, give good tidings to them that ask him?

Since I was so ignorant of the Word, it took at least 10 hours of perpetration for one hour of teaching. However, this was very good for me and forced me to understand the Word.

Brother Larry again was the most brilliant preacher, who went into the Greek word meanings or words and phrases' taught me a lot about studying the Word. I had purchased a Strong's Concordance, a set of Mathew Hendry's Commentary, Wuest Word Studies in the Greek, and many other books to learn more about God's word. I purchased and gave away several different sets of these books to others in the Church at that time to get a better understanding of the Word of God. I do not mention this to build myself up but to point out that there was a hunger to understand the Word of God. Others used the books to teach their Sunday School classes to open the bread of life to those they taught.

Before the world's foundation, there was the Word, and the Word was with God (Jesus). Therefore, in God's mind, who cannot lie, had already laid down his only son, part of himself for **MY** sins. Always make it personal.

Why wasn't the Lord letting me build my dream home?

Now every one of my relatives had already sold their old home, but I could not sell mine. I was teaching Sunday school and doing all that I knew to do for my Lord at that time. Yet, I could not build my new dream home. I was wondering and doubting God. What was going on? I was doing everything right. Giving my time and money to my Lord, yet others were getting the homes of their dreams built. Why wasn't I? I believed I deserved it more than the others. I remember questioning my Lord many times about this situation. Have you ever been in this situation?

Do others seem to be blessed who did not deserve to be blessed?

I believed the Lord used this experience to teach me a lesson that I did not understand. Only through hindsight, many of the tasks my Lord was trying to teach me, did I finally understand. If I could have only comprehended what he was trying to teach me, I could have missed many disappointments and heartache in my journey through life. I already had drawn my plans up from my design. I saved a little money, cleared the area, and filled and poured the floor. I was able to do a lot of this work myself. I finally saved up enough funds to pored the floor and put up the block walls and the tie beam. The rest of the family had completed their homes and lived in them by now. I went to the property of my future home almost daily. I helped and built some of my relative's homes since I was in the Construction business at the time. Why were they being blessed, and I was not? I was living for my Lord; some of them were not?

How I met Carol Ford, a rock mason who did all the rock work in my home: Later, God used him in the most incredible miracles I have ever experienced in my entire life.

The block walls and tie-beam on my new dream home stood there for at least a year. The area was all weeded up. Then, as I recall, I was there, one day and this person drove up in an old red beat-up truck. He looked to be a wine O. He was asking for work. How he knew I needed any help is still a mystery to me. He did not look to me as if he could do anything. Anyway, I talked with him and showed him the home's layout. I was going to build two fireplaces in my house. He said he could make them.

I had already priced the labor and materials with others, and they wanted $5,000.00 each in labor to build them. Remember, I was in the construction business at that time. I have had several fireplaces built in other homes by subcontractors.

It is a long and complicated story, but you will understand one of the **greatest <u>MIRACLES</u>**, which continues to bring tears of joy to my eyes every time I tell it to someone. So hang in there with me, I will get to the point, but the background is significant to understand this miracle.

Background for the MIRACLE of Carol Ford, the rock mason:

When **Carol Ford**, do not forget this name, told me he would build my Rock fireplaces for $500.00 each, I took note. I thought to myself, I had to purchase the rock and material anyway, which was not that expensive, why not give him the chance to build them. If he could not do it, what did I have to lose? The rocks would be needed later anyway, whoever built the fireplaces. I would save a lot of money. I did not know if he could build a birdhouse based on personal looks. Later in life, I have often wondered if he was not an angel sent by God.

So here we go, fast forward into the future. Carol Ford built two of the best-looking rock fireplaces I have ever seen. One was over 10' high, to the ceiling in the living room and about 15' wide, and the other one in the family room was 20' wide and 8' tall with rock planters on the sides to dived from the kitchen the family room.

Now I had the floor, block walls, tie beam, and two beautiful rock fireplaces, and which just set there for a long time before I sold my old home and was able to build my dream home. Of course, my dream home is not essential, but the fireplaces are, since later God will use this experience in building his Church on the "Promised Land." Remember, at this time, I was not aware of the task God was preparing me for in the future.

Once we completed our dream home, we used it for Sunday School class meetings, cookouts, a place for visiting evangelists to stay while preaching in revivals at both the old and new church buildings.

I believe that God's leadership was in the building of my fireplaces in hindsight. The idea of a rock wall behind the pulpit area with beams holding the rocks in place.

Below is a picture of the fireplace in my family room. Carol Ford built it in my home in 1984. Try to picture this fireplace with only a blank block wall behind it.

Below is a side view picture of the family room fireplace.

This picture is of the Living room fireplace built by Carol Ford after the home was finished. Picture it as standing alone in the middle of the house with nothing behind it. We built the room around the fireplace.

Now let's move forward many years in the future. I am at the entrance of building the Church building. I had designed a lot of rockwork to be done in the church.

I could not locate a rock mason anywhere to lay the rocks for the new church building:

I remember this as if it just happened today. I could not locate a brick/rock mason to lay the Foyers' rocks and the rock wall behind the pulpit. I had looked everywhere, phoned several masons I had used in the past. This part of the building process could hold up to the following stages. I looked and looked, called, and called. I was in the foyer area of the sanctuary one day. I remember saying to my father, who I talked to a lot as if he was standing beside me, while I was in the sanctuary's Foyer that I would give anything to know where **Carol Ford** was.

Within minutes, if not seconds, and I believe seconds is the best description, Carol Ford, a wine O I thought, walked into the Foyer at the First Baptist Church in Immokalee.

I practiced talking to my Lord as if he was my earthly father and as if he was walking beside me throughout the day. You should try it.

> *Matthew 7: V. 7-V11: if ye then being evil, know how to give good gifts unto your children, how much more shall your Father who is in heaven give good things to them that ask him.*

This picture is of the foyer where I was standing at that time. There was only a wood cross with no rocks were not there yet. When I was talking to God, I asked him, "Where is Carol Ford"?

Next is the picture of the doors where Carol Ford walked through instantly after I asked God where he was. "ANOTHER MIRACLE"

May my God Strike me dead if this is not the truth. Try to tell me that this was not an incredible **MIRACLE**. I had no idea where on earth Carol Ford was. He appeared or walked in. I am not sure which since; I did not see him walk into the building. After looking at the wood cross that Melvin Taylor had built, I just turned around in the Foyer. I wondered who I would get to install the rock around the cross. Within an instant, Carol Ford appeared in the doorway to inside the foyer.

The **Carol Ford, MIRACLE,** is one the strongest I have ever seen in my life. It was a physical miracle that happened to me alone in the Church's Foyer when I asked God in my mind in prayer for help. But it is not the best one. As I continue this true story, there is one more, even more, powerful to me, which I will get into later.

Carol Ford is done with the Rockwork and left. I still do not know where he came from or where he went. I still wonder if he was an angel or a man. Probably a man God used, but I still wonder. This is one question of many I would like to ask when I get to heaven.

The points or truths I am trying to make here are several. **First**, I believe the Lord used my personal home-building experiences to lead me, Carol Ford. **Second**, God used his foreknowledge to cause these events to happen in the past to lead me to the person he wanted to be used to lay the rocks in his Church. Neither Carol Ford nor I knew when he showed up at my dream home that he or I would be used in the building of God's Church on the "Promised Land." **Third**, and most importantly, it reassures me, and it should also reassure others, especially the church of 2013 the Promised Land is a Holly property, as Brother Babb Adams believed. The property should never be sold or used for any other purpose.

This fact strengthened my belief that the Lord had been planning to build his church on the Promised Land for many years. In his all-seeing and all-knowing, the events needed to occur in a definite order to build His Church building and sent Carol Ford, an alcoholic, to me two times when I needed him. Of course, the most important was the building for the Church, but I would have never listened, considered, or trusted him with doing all the rockwork at the First Baptist Church of Immokalee if I did not have the first experience with Carol Ford.

This MIRACLE is one of the main reasons I believe so strongly that Satan wishes to destroy the First Baptist Church of Immokalee. As I also know, Satan knows that the Lord took a particular interest in building the church on the Promised Land. Satan will use any method possible to destroy the "Promised Land." Holly Land, I believe, that God himself wanted it built, and Satan wants to destroy it. I cannot believe that God would have made so many events happen in a definite order to make the building of His Church possible. I cannot believe that God would have done all this just for his Church to exist for only a few years on the "Promised Land."

THE MEMBERS OF THE FIRST BAPTIST CHURCH NEED TO STAY ON GUARD AGAINST ANYONE WANTING TO DESTROY THE "**PROMISED LAND.**"

This is why I believe the members of the First Baptist Church must fight to the last second to save the "Promised Land." But most of all, do all they can first, be doers of the Word, not just hearers, as the book of James teaches, and then trust the Lord to work another **Miracle** to save his Church on the "Promised Land." However, the members need to be careful not just sit and wait for the Lord to work. I believe that our Lord expects us to do all we can first. That is one of his conditions before he acts with his Miracles. He requires us to step out first with our faith.

There must be some significant event in the future why the Lord performed so many miracles to make the "**Promised Land**" possible and have his Church built upon it.

Again, the Carol Ford miracle that was so real in human experience and physical, something you could see and touch, was one of the most memorable to me. But there still was another Miracle, one greater that all the people in Immokalee witnessed, which I will get to later.

I prayed for rain, and it rained. Miracle:

There was another one in my life when I had decided to burn an area behind my new dream home, which may have conditioned me and given me the experience and faith to ask God, my father, for help in times of real need. The Bible teaches us to ask our father for what we need. He is a good father and wants to help. I suggest that all Christians walk daily and talk daily with their heavenly father. He knows your actual need and will provide the best for you if you will only trust him.

It was a clear sunny day. I decided to burn a ditch bank behind my recently completed dream home on 10 acres. The fire got away from me. The wind picked up in a direction that sent the fire directly towards my dream home, just completed. I tried to put it out. I was almost going to have a stroke, trying to put it out. It was headed directly towards my new dream home. There was no time to phone anyone. I do not recall any cell phones at that time. I prayed or asked out loud, Lord, please let it rain to control this fire. I cannot do it. Within seconds on this fine, clear day with no clouds in sight, it started to rain. The rain put the fire out and then suddenly stopped.

James 5: 17-18: Elijah was a man subject to like passions as we are, and he prayed earnestly that it might not rain, and it rained not on the earth by the space of three years and six months. V 18: And he prayed again, the heaven gave rain, and the earth brought forth her fruit.

Furthermore, this is the total truth; all the events in this book happened. I was alone, and no one else experienced this **Miracle** but me. This experience gave me the confidence to ask the Lord for help in a great time of need, talk with him as if he was my father with honor and glory, but talk with him. If God had not intervened, my dream home would have been burnt to the ground. God saving my dream home was an extraordinary Miracle. I believed it was in God's strategy to go through these trials in my life's journey to prepare me for future events.

I am sure that God directed my life and will also direct yours. He intervenes many times even when we do not ask him to. But our lives will be fuller of joy if we communicate with our Lord as our Heavenly Father, who loves to hear from us in prayer and just plain meditation and to talk to him as our father. Having fellowship with him

MIRACLE: Be still, listen to the Lord, and Wait for the Lord to Act.

Satan throws his last fiery dart in 1986 to destroy the building project on Promised Land.

We are finished with the first construction phase, building one, the Sanctuary. It is time to apply for the sanctuary Certificate of Occupancy, the C O, called in the building industry. With the C O, you can get your permit for the Electric Company to hook up the electric service. So we were ready for that part of the building phase. The Family life center was also almost finished. But we needed the C O to get the electricity turned on in the sanctuary to check all the electrical items, sound systems, and many other details.

At that time, I was trying to get my pilot's license. I needed to fly back and forth from Immokalee to the Keys, where I had business interests. It was time for me to go to Panama City to a prescheduled flight school. I had already set up the county inspectors to do the final inspection. Therefore, I went to flight school; confident everything was good to go.

My friend Steve Price had flown me up there and picked me up after flight school in a few days. So I was sure that everything in the building would check out, and we would get the C O.

I got a message from Steve from the flight school office that I needed to phone him ASAP. Satan attacks again with his last fiery dart. Steve tells me that the county will not approve the C O because we do not have enough parking. There wasn't anything wrong with the construction, by the rules or regulations set by the county codes at that time, and they approved the plans.

I am distraught and in tears in a phone booth in Panama City. I asked Steve to come to pick me up ASAP, forget the flight School. Instead, Steve convinced me to stay there and finish school and work things out when I got back. I passed the pilot's test, unsure how, with the Church building on my mind, and then headed back to Immokalee to work on this issue.

The county had decided to measure the square footage of the entire buildings. They did not consider that the Sunday School classrooms, gym, and sanctuary would never be used simultaneously. They said that we did not have enough parking based upon the total square footage of both buildings. Anyone using common sense would recognize that the sanctuary and Sunday school rooms would not be used simultaneously; therefore, there was plenty of parking space.

Of course, common sense does not rule anymore but only legalist rules and regulations.

Remember, the County had already approved the site plan, including the parking area for both buildings. So we could not have gotten a building permit without it initially?

The county wanted us to double the asphalt parking lot in size, and then they would give us the C O. **Jack Queen** donated the parking lot paving for the entire site. The parking area was rarely full. Maybe if there was a high-priority community funeral, there might have been a minor overflow, but we had several acres of grass parking available in that case. So the whole idea was just simply the final dart that Satan could use to stop the Promise Land.

It was a vast and damaging dart cast by Satan. According to the county official, we would have completely removed all the parking lot asphalt, redesigned the water drainage and the landscaping, and doubled the size of everything.

The fact was, we did not need the additional parking. I worked and worked talking by phone to those in Naples, where the county seat controlled everything at that time. I could not convince them to use their common sense. They said we had to double the parking. It was no way but their way. This meant we could not get electricity, and we would have to redesign the total parking lot. Remove all the pants and scrubs. <u>After all, remember the county had already approved the site plan for the entire building plan that the parking lot was part of</u>. To me, this was a Satan attack issue.

It was one of his last efforts to stop the building from opening. So why now bring this up. The county had already approved the site plans. Tear up the brand new parking lot and redesign it. Redesign all the drainage plans. This would take months. It was not necessary. I knew

Above is a picture of part of the Parking lot around three sides of the buildings on the Promised Land. The picture was taken in 2020.

there was something else going on here, a spiritual battle between Satan and my Lord.

I finally had enough, and I requested to meet with the head building official about this issue in Naples, our county seat. I thought at that time my interpreter, Mosses, and Aron Concept, Steve Price, could go, but he could not make the meeting for some reason. In God's foreknowledge, it was best. Steve and I had similar feelings toward those in power who would not use common sense. I could not understand why?

But now I was in trouble because Steve could not go to the meeting. I was in real danger now. I was very bitter and angry about this stupid decision about the parking lot. I had experienced it many other times in the construction business. Nothing makes me madder than dealing with educated idiots only reading regulations and not using common sense in making their decisions. I was not the right person to be alone when dealing with them. But now, I was faced with meeting the building official alone. I was not sure I could communicate with him and control anger and emotions.

Another <u>Miracle obtaining the C O</u>: One of our Deacons, Gary Bates, was able to go, and the Lord used him

Somehow the Lord, <u>I know</u>, again stepped in and performed another **Miracle** because the Lord teamed me up with Gary Bates. Remember Steve Price and my personalities were very similar and very strong about officials in any office not using common sense. Gary was a good and great Godly man and deacon friend. It was in Gary's natural or God-given talent to be a peacemaker. He was good at communicating with others. He went with me to the Building Official meeting. We sat down in Naples together with a building official. I do not believe it was the head building inspector for the county. I explained our position and reasoning as written above. We seemed not to be getting anywhere. I was hot, frustrated, upset, and angry, ready to battle and go to all-out war.

Here we go to the meeting with a county person. Gary did not say much if anything. But he calmed me down and gave me confidence that our Lord would work this out. I was going on and on, not letting the county person talk much. I was unsure who the county repetitive was; the man said one time, "Morris, I am trying to help you." I did not understand the true meaning of those words. I thought he was just trying to be clever. "Those who have ears let them hear."

Here I went again, on and on; The County cannot do this. Please use common sense, not just reading regulations out of a book. Do you want 250 Baptist and all of Immokalee in a rage about this stupid decision?? Again, the man said calmly, "Morris, I am trying to help you." I still did not hear the meaning of those words, and here I go again, very upset. I still thought that he was not honest with me.

The man said again, "Morris, I am trying to help you" I am now finally hearing his words but wondering what that means. "Those who have ears listen." In most of my experience in the past dealing with building officials, that meant the opposite.

Gary calmed me down and said something to the effect, let the man talk and listen. I finally heard what Gary and the county building official for inspections were saying, shut up, and became still. He signed off on the permit on the building, saying, "after all, there was enough parking for the first building, correct? if you did not add the second building into the plan, right?". So you are not asking for the C O for the second building at this time, correct?

Psalms 46: V.10: Be still, and know that I am God: I will be exalted among the nations, I will be exalted in the earth

I am not sure who brought this idea up, Gary, me, or the County person. But I believe it is the one idea that the county official had already made up his mind that he could approve even before we started the meeting. I think that he must have been a Christian person who listened to his Lord. Maybe he did not want 250 Baptist, upset with and coming to Naples, the county office, to protest.

I have no idea if that is true, but we had our C. O. The electric company was permitted to connect to the building within minutes. I do not believe this event happen by accident. I had tried hard to talk with someone who had common sense and would not just look in the rule book to base their decision. God, I believe, arranged things so Steve could not go and had Gary already prepared to take his place. **ANOTHER MIRACLE**. God had prearranged that we would meet with a particular building official who was willing to give us the C. O.

This true story attests to the fact, I believe that we have to do all we can do on our own, and then God will work his **Miracles**. Again, this story points out that we were doers, as the Book of James points out. We did everything possible to get the C. O. We were getting nowhere, yet we did not give up. We were persistent. We kept doing all we could do.

By the way, Gary Bates was the only Deacon Brother who showed concern and visited me when I was going through some terrible financial times and personal issues of loss of faith in our Lord a few years later in my walk through life. He visited me when I was having problems with many of my Christian brothers and a particular deacon brother, who had let me down, some of which helped to cause my finical destruction in my farming ventures at that time.

Gary never took sides and would not talk against his Christian Brothers. He only showed concern and love, and compassion for me.

Gary was a very compassionate man of God and is now in a much better place. But, unfortunately, he passed at a very young age. He would still be with us if I had my will. God should have taken me instead of him. But I must trust my Lord that he knows best and must have needed Gary Bates in heaven for some particular reason.

I often have to wonder why to take Gary a much better person than I am. I miss him. He was a great man of God. So I guess I can answer my question like this. God needed me to help save his Promised Land in the future, which was the main reason for writing this book in 2013.

MIRACLE of the Halo over the entire Church property for hours: Well done thou good and faithful servants, from 1916 to completing his Church 1986.

Now let us move forward. I am almost at the end of this true story. The best **MIRACLE**, which was seen by all, is about to happen.

O C is issued. The electricity is on. We are doing the final touches on the church. The family Life center construction has been completed. My wife and I, Reece, Marty, my sons were just little boys, but they can still remember it. My wonderful wife and high school sweetheart and all of us were picking up the paper in the yard between the sanctuary and the family life center. I looked up, and there was a Halo over the entire church building. There was not any rain in sight. It was Not a rainbow from horizon to horizon, which we have all seen many times before, but a halo. It looked like a crown over the top of both buildings.

The colors were gold, yellow, and green. It circled and hovered over the Church buildings. It could be seen by anyone in Immokalee traveling east or west or north or south. It was not there for only minutes, but it remained there for hours. I had never seen anything like it in my life. I believe it stayed there all day. From the time I have seen it in the early morning, about 9 am until late afternoon. I wished I had taken a picture of it. It was a fantastic sight.

Recently I mentioned this event to Bennie Zipperer in 2013. He also recalls the event. I am wondering how many others in our Church family remembered the Halo. If you are a past member of the First Baptist Church in 1986, I would appreciate it if you would contact me if you witnessed this advent. My e/mail address is Morris@mainadvent.com. I believe that the Church of 2013 must know about this Advent. Remembering this advent should encourage them and strengthen their faith as we battle bad events on the horizon in their personal lives. We should have faith that God is with us when facing conflicts we cannot foresee. When you read about the real-life miracles building of the Church on the "Promised Land," It will increase your faith.

Now try to tell me this is not a **MIRACLE**. It was not a natural event. It was as if, when we were done with the building and ready for the first Church service, that the Lord was saying, "Well done though good and faithful servants." <u>I know</u> that he spoke directly to my family and me that day. Also, to those who were 75- 100 years before us, and until that present time, we all had followed his will. I believe the Lord was pleased with the faith of his church and with his building.

This picture Illustrates where my family and I were picking up trash, where suddenly a Halo over the entire Church building appeared the day before the first church service.

After the Church was completed and functioning. Brother Daryl Alexander (1986-1991) becomes the first Pastor at

the New Church building at the corner of Lake Trafford and highway 29.

Now both buildings are completed. We continued to have an interim pastor. All the plans we had made were now in operation. We had new classrooms for Sunday school, a new sanctuary for worship, a family life center with a professional high school basketball court for our young to enjoy, a complete and modern kitchen, professional ovens and stoves, and an eating area for us to enjoy family fellowship times together. Wow-what great times of fellowship and togetherness we shared in those days. I have never experienced anything like it in any other period in any other church I have ever attended. So many were led to the Lord in the church on Highway 29 and in the new facility. Several dedicated their lives to becoming pastors and preachers in several years, just before the building started.

Our Lord now sends the exact personality style of pastor that our church body needed to set the new foundation for his Church. Brother Daryl Alexandra was a great man of God. He has passed and gone to be with our Lord. He was a man of Love, emotion, compassion, and understanding. He was perfect for the needs of our church at that time, replacing Brother Larry, who had a youthful and dominant personality. He was the exact person we needed for our Church. We had an interim pastor for the two years we were in the building process. The church had a different need, and the Lord called a man full of love and compassion Brother Daryl. He was the Shepherd we needed at this time. Brother Larry was the best

Bible scholar and preacher I have ever had the pleasure to listen to.

Brother Daryl was the most outstanding pastor who showed love and compassion that I have ever had the privilege to know. Both were perfect for the needs of the Church as per God's plan. I was a very close friend to both of them and took them to the Keys to fish with me.

Brother Daryl's sermons were full of love, kindness, and compassion. He believed the words in the following verse.

> *Romans 2:4: Or despises thou the riches of his goodness and forbearance, and long-suffering, not knowing that the goodness of God leadeth thee to repentance?*

I am not sure how the Lord works in your life, but in mine, the way he gets my attention is that when I do something terrible, and I know it is awful when I do it, that the Lord will do something extraordinary good in my life which I do not deserve. He gives me good things when I sin, which I do not deserve. It makes me ashamed of how I could let down such a loving Father. It convicts me and drives me to repentance. I believe My Lord, at least in my own life, uses this technique first. It was the attitude and motivation of the sermons of Brother Daryl.

I understand that the Lord will also use another method to Chastens those he loves to bring us back into his will. I was also proving that he loves us as a Father.

Romans 12: verse 6-15: verse 11: "Now no chastening for the present seemeth to be joyous, but grievous, nevertheless, afterward it, yieldeth the peaceable fruit of righteousness unto them who are exercised by it"

Both of these techniques are effective depending upon which has more effect on your life. But I believe Romans. 2:4 is our Lord's preferred choice of motivating us.

Later, Brother Daryl thought his ministry was over and left to go to another Church. Notice the Lord directed Brother Larry and Brother Daryl's attitude towards staying at a Church. They both followed what they believed was the Lord's will. When the Lord told them their job was finished, they surrendered to their Lord's will, unlike some other pastors who believe they should stay in the same pulpit no matter what state the Church is in.

In my opinion, they are saying that they do not care what the will of our Lord is. It is an entirely different attitude than all the other pastors of God whom I have known, Brother Babb Adams, Brother Larry Finley, and Brother Daryl Alexander.

After Brother Daryl Alexander as pastor in Immokalee, who left in 1991, my life and family's life changed dramatically. From 1992 to 2000 was a very troubling time for my family and me. I have already talked about this period early in this book.

Others will have to write about the church's history from 1993 to 2013. Some of that history is on the First Baptist Church of Immokalee website.

Hopefully, some will read this book, and it will renew their spirit with reassurance and understand that your Father will never leave you in your life's journey. It is us that leave God. He never leaves us. As you have read part of my life's journey, I hope you will understand that God is also walking with you in your Journey. I pray that the real, touchable, seeable miracles written about will increase your faith. Let me encourage you, if you have separated yourself from your Heavenly Father, that you return to him now. He will be glad to welcome you back home.

Let me encourage you to return to your loving Father. Do not let Satan deceive you as he did me for many years. God did not forget me, even though I had falsely blamed him, thinking he had abandoned me. I have concluded from this true story about my Journey points out the fact that God had not left me. He was and is always there. All the events written about in this book continually prove that God was always there preparing the way. He has not abandoned you either. God will never do that. All we have to do is repent, and he will hear your prayers again.

Satan deceives us in our mind and heart, and we begin to doubt our Heavily Father Love. If we do not control our, **TO Will**, a gift for God discussed earlier in the book, we will begin to doubt our Father. We will become like the Children of Israel and walk through life's journey in the wilderness, 40 years, trying to get to the Promised Land.

We will become like the 12 spies written about earlier. The Irony of this true story is that they were only forty miles from the Promised Land promised them from time. We were only 30 plus miles from the same building, which most at one time many did not believe we could build. So they began to doubt and separate themselves from God. They wasted years of not being happy and enjoying the blessing that God had already prepared for them.

Please learn from these stories and hopefully from the actual experiences in this book that God loves us and will always be with us and will never depart from us even when bad things happen. Also, no matter what happens, God is in control, and he will always turn bad things into good things for those who love him and are called for his purpose.

When I think about my wilderness walk, I am ashamed of what I might have been able to have done for my Heavily Father during that period. I will have to give an account to him at his Judgment Seat. But I cannot focus on these facts, nor should you. I must continue to renew my mind in the words of Romans 5:8 that <u>while I was yet a sinner, Christ died for me</u>, as stated earlier in this book. God already knows the sins we will commit even before we are saved. He has already forgiven these sins even before we have committed them, **amazing Grace**. We must do what Romans 12: 1-2 states and be transformed by renewing our minds and focusing on how much God loved us that he sent his Son, Jesus, to die a horrible death on the Cross for us.

We must again focus on good positive thoughts in our minds about the love of God. First, we need to read his Word daylily and be in constant prayer. Then, read the book about positive thinking by Norman Vince Peale.

This book should give you something to latch on to, which will provide you with a better understanding of how God worked in your life. That he still loves us no matter what we do or how much we fail in our life. Do not let this separate you from God's Love. Remember David was a murderer, yet God also called him a Man of his own heart, **Amazing Grace**.

I now understand that even though I have failed my Lord in many ways, he still loves me. So, therefore, when I get my heart right with him, he can still use us for the good of this kingdom.

One of the best ways to do this is to join a Bible Believing Church of your choice. Then, associate yourself with other believers.

I hope you will remember the Journey in Life is long, challenging, and stressful, especially if you do not have a relationship with Jesus. Even if you do, God has never promised, as some preachers do, life will be easy just because you are a believer. Jesus told his disciples to count the cost before they joined him.

God has a plan for your life, and it may not be what you wanted, but the facts about my personal life (Lord, not thy Will but My Will and the perfect gift of the most incredible women in the world my Dolls) story written about earlier. It should give you the understanding to accept God's will for your life. It is best for you. Learn to accept your circumstances and trust God. He is faithful to lead you in the right direction. It is not an easy task. Satan will continue to toss his fiery darts at you every day.

When you begin to have doubts about the love of God, latch onto **Miracles** that happen in your own life. <u>Sing the song Count your many blessings name them one by one, see what God has done</u>. Do you have your eyesight? Can you walk? Think about all those around you that have many more negative and stressful issues in their lives than you do. Think about those Dolores Blackburns you have to know in your life journey, which was written earlier in this book.

If you do not have any that you can remember, I am sure that you really can if you try to remember the Miracles that happened on my journey to the Promised Land. The touchable, seeable, tangible, physical Miracles that occur that I have written about in the book. Also, remember that life is about the Journey to your Promised Land. The examples that I have written about should bring to your mind times in your own life where God has done things or caused events to change your path, and throughout your entire life, he has been trying to lead you in the right direction.

We are concluding the Journey to the "Promised Land": The History of building the First Baptist Church of Immokalee. However, this is not the final chapter since this is a continuing story.

I understand there will be many doubters of this true story. However, I believe all these details are accurate, especially those that I experienced. The fact is I know that it is all true. I may have a few dates and details confused, but that is not even the most critical part of this true story and history. I am sure my spelling and grammar are not proper, but that is not an essential part of this story. I am just a simple man trying to do what the Lord has compelled me to do. I have spent many hours over many years revising and writing this story.

I am sure the Church built on the "Promised Land" will continue. Although at the time of the original writing in 2013, there was a solid movement to destroy it.

Remember, God does not always have his perfect followed. If that were true, none would be lost, and all would go to heaven. Nevertheless, the 2013 edition helped renew the faith in God's raiment to save the Promised Land from destruction. The revision in 2020 will give all believers understanding and encouragement to face the events in our new future.

Understanding all this, I still believe it is my Father's will to continue writing this story. Even include some of the adverse events in this book about the "Promised Land" journey. I hope that someone may use this book to help them increase their faith. Or maybe it will help another church grow their confidence in their building project.

I have set this book aside many times, wondering if all this writing will have any purpose. I was wondering who will edit it? Who will publish it? The fiery darts of the devil continue to hit me. Even my wife sometimes makes fun of me when I take our time together. However, she is very supportive and encourages me for the most part. Other issues continue to enter my mind and soul. Satan continues with those fiery darts are causing many personal life problems, age, mental and physical pain, and many doubts. Yet, for some reason, I continually come back to this book and add more and more to it as I believe the Lord inspires me too.

When I think I am finished writing this book, some delay happens. I keep wondering why I continue to be delayed in completing it. I continue reviewing it and editing the grammar. But for some reason, I can not finish the book. I can not complete the last few pages. I have been praying to God, why can I not get to the end and send it on to a publisher. An editor has requested that I send a copy to them many times, yet something seems to be missing.

I think I have finally have gotten my answer. I believed there was just something more that God wanted me to add. I become aware of recent events that should be in this book.

On Sept. 26, 2020, a gathering in Washington D. C. called the National and Global Day of Prayer and Repentance. The day when 50,000 or more Christians gathered together to pray for our country. One of the speakers was Johanna Cahn. I had never heard him before, but his speech was incredible. You could call it a sermon if you want. I strongly suggest you listen to it on the internet at thereturn.org. Open it then; It starts 3.02 minutes into the video in the part one 540 minute section of the return on this website. You first click on Part 1, then after it loads, click at the top of the video, click again, and scan to 3.02 minutes. It is a must-listen for all Christians. He talks about the return with many historical facts that will bless your soul and faith. He must be a Jewish Rabi who speaks and understands the Hebrew language. He goes back to the history of Israel 2500 years ago, reading the original Hebrew words, and compares those events to the events today in 2020. He uses the story of a sermon to the Children of Israel about the .potter's clay vessel. It centers upon the verse, THE RETURN

2 Chronicles 7:14 IF my people called by my name shall HUMBLE themselves, and PRAY, and SEEK my face, and TURN from their wicked ways THEN I WILL HEAR, from heaven, and will forgive their sin, and will HEAL THEIR LAND.

There is too much information in this video to write about in this book, but I must mention at least three things. First, when they scheduled this event, focusing on turning back to God, on Sept. 26, it was on the exact date of the Jewish Holiday called the Festival of the Return, celebrated 1000s of years ago.

Second, the location chosen was the National Mall which was the same place that our forefathers committed to God that America would be founded on him and his principles.

Third, during his sermon, there is thunder in the background. Mr. Cahn makes a reference that God talks through thunder. It reminded me of my story when I asked God for rain, written earlier in this book.

Again, please take time to listen to this message to ALL; I GUARANTEE YOU WILL BE HAPPY THAT YOU DID.

Next, only a few days later, in the same week, on Oct. 1, 2020, I turned on the TV by chance Newsmax TV. An advertisement related to an earlier part of the book. When I wrote about proving the Bible is confirmed by using prophecy. Remember the chip. I just turned on the TV, and within seconds Amazon puts out an ad that says **"IN THE PALM OF YOUR HAND"**. We will soon be purchasing from them by just waving your hand over your phone or computer.

> *Revelation 14:17: And that no man might buy or sell, except he that had the mark or the name of the beast, or the number of his name.*
>
> *20:4: ...had received his Mark upon their foreheads, or their HANDS*

I continue the fight and sin and do things like Paul, and I know not what I do? Nor why I continue to sin? I fail to use my **Will and** make wrong decisions. I continue to fight the flesh as we all do. But I believe the Lord does not want me to use that excuse and continue the race and finish this book.

Thank God for his limitless in his mercy and forgiveness. Satan often tempts me, saying to my mind, you are such a sinner. How can you believe that God continues to talk to you? Yet when these things happen, God speaks to my heart and reminds me that even David had sin in his life in the Old Testament, and even Paul had issues with sin.

Nothing would get done if we did not do God's will just because we were sinners. God knew I was a sinner before he saved me. He knew already that I would continue to sin ever before he saved me. For we are all Sinners and come very short compared to the Glory of God.

Therefore, I cannot use this excuse not to stop writing and do what I believe my Father wants me to do.

This book may only be helpful to me to renew my faith in my Father and Lord. The story in this book would make a great Christian movie. Who knows what will happen in the future.

I hope this true story will increase those who love the Lord's faith to give them the courage to stand alone. I hope that the many side streets as I walked through life with my Father and Lord will be helpful examples of true-life situations to others were walking with their father. They are also hoping that others will relate and remember how our Lord has walked with them throughout their life. These side streets may cause readers to recognize times and events in their own lives when Jesus was walking with them, and they were not aware of it.

That maybe it will be of help to those who are facing Church issues and give them the courage to listen to their hearts and read the word, and search for the truth and not be blinded sheep following those who do not have faith to trust our Lord that Miracles still happen today.

I believe that this book will:

First, help those Church members in Immokalee to understand their history and the sacrifices of many over 100 years to become a reality.

Second, the many MIRACLES that happen during the facility's planning and building process should be remembered. They should give all Christians strength and courage to finish the course and protect the Promised Land that many others have done before them.

Third, to give them and other Christians the understanding that Satan did not in history want the "Promised Land" to exist and would do anything to destroy it then and in the future.

Fourth, God will work his MIRACLES to save the Church and help other Christians, only if the members do all they can on their own first, not waiting on God to do everything for them.

Fifth, God used many different people, the members in his Church, all with different God-given talents/gifts. Most of them had minor skills. Everyone should understand how God works over many years. He was causes events and experiences in our lives to prepare us for the task he has for us to do. God works in the same way today.

God has always loved to use the unusable and makes them useable confidence to do his work so that God will get all the Glory.

God is walking beside every Christian in everyday life experiences. We just have to open our eyes to see it. "Practice the Presents" of God as Brother Babb Adams referred to it. Sometimes we can only see by hindsight, but foresight and hindsight are essential for Christians to understand their walk through life with their Father in heaven.

Sixth, God often uses simple things in our journey through life to reach our personal "Promised Land". Thus, he prepares Christians for their final Promised Land, Heaven.

Seventh, God loves us and is with us always. If we are saved, he never leaves us, even if we leave him. God is always providing an opportunity to return to his will. He rejoices, and the angels in heaven rejoice when a prodigal son returns. That God first uses positive kind undeserving events in our life to get us to repent and turn back to him.

But it is also true that God will chasten those children who are his, who will not repent and turn back to him.

Eight, that all Christians will have to stand at the Judgment and give an accounting of their life. Jack Van Impi wrote a great article about how we will feel if we do not have any crowns to give to our Lord at the Judgment seat of Christ. Will you be one of those who have lost their crowns and be ashamed of the number of crowns you have to give to our Lord at the Judgment seat to prove to him that you truly loved him and appreciated what he did for you? I pray that my Father will open your heart and mind as you read this book and let it speak to your soul that you will remember who you are and to whom you serve. I pray that this book will revive your spirit, knowing that your Father is involved and concerned with your daily walk, your Journey, with him to your "Promised Land" heaven. It is the destiny of our final Journey to our last home, the Promised Land in Heaven, and to be with Jesus our Lord for eternity.

I pray that this book will renew your hunger for God's word, and you will study it, "be ye transfer by and renewing your minds" as Romans Chapter 12. Verses 1-2 teach.

Even now, I pray that all understand I did not write this to build myself up. It has taken hundreds of others to make the dream of the PROMISE LAND possible. It is not something I wanted to do. But as I have stated before, I felt compelled to do so. I hope and pray that I have not offended anyone in the writings in this book. I did not intend to leave anyone out who did work to get the First Baptist Church to the "Promised Land."

Some may have wished that their influence and actions were not made public. My intent was not to hurt them in any way be to build them up and give them praise for letting the Lord use them in the Journey to the "Promised Land." I believe at this particular time in the history of the First Baptist Church of Immokalee, especially concerning the events in 2013, considering selling the Promised Land, although bad at the time worked for good.

I do understand that some may have different conclusions than the ones I have. I hope those will give careful and prayerful consideration to the details I have written about.

My heart and mind, and thoughts are with you continually.

The original manuscript was given to several different members of the First Baptist Church of Immokalee in 2013. The deacons who had an essential role in reaching the Promised Land during the 1980s and the two pastors who witnessed and experienced the events.

Brother Babb Adams, Brother Larry Finley, and Brother Tim, the present pastor in 2020, were also given a copy. Brother Adams and Brother Larry strongly suggested I get it published and, of course, professionally edited. I cannot help but believe it did significantly influence saving the Promised Land from destruction in 2013.

The Promised Land was saved from destruction in 2013 by small raiment.

God did raise a small raiment of Christian members of the Church, maybe 10-15 of members who did take a stand, worked together, and overturned the contract to Sell the Promised Land. I believe that this book's writing helps them understand the importance of the Promised Land and how special it is.

Many of the original members of the Church decided to leave the Church. Many were just tired of the division within the Church. I cannot blame them and completely understand why they left and went to other Churches in the area. I have no ill will towards them. But I thank God that a few were willing to continue the race, finish the course, and fight to save the Promised Land.

None of them want any credit. However, they should be remembered because there would not be a church today on the Promised Land in Immokalee if they had not taken a stand.

Yes, the Church is still there today, functioning and still in the business of saving souls. It has started another mission from another town close by where souls were also saved. The original Church, the Promised Land, is still shining bright for the people of Immokalee. The new Pastor in late 2015 has taken a different approach to a multicultural welcoming all races to feel as if they are home. I believe this is the correct approach for the Church to continue to function.

I am sure the Church will have issues to deal with, as most Churches today have. However, I hope and pray that they will never again consider destroying and selling the Promised

Land. I do not believe they will ever consider selling the Promised Land again. But if they do, I also believe God will raise another witness to protect his Holly Promised Land.

I hope and pray all the members of the First Baptist Church in Immokalee, when they voted to sell the Promised Land in 2013 on both sides of the issue, will forgive one another if they have any hard feelings with any of their Christian brothers and sisters. I hope none will hold against me hard feelings as I believe truly in my heart that I did do what the Lord wanted me to do to help save his Promised Land.

I understand that many had different views than I and a few others did. Some left the Church because a few decided to take a stand for what they believed. Church member and pastor differences happen all the time. It is sad to say. More people leave the Church for this reason than any other. It is not what Jesus taught us.

Leaving your church is not a good thing. Most that stop going to church also leave the Lord and quit communicating with their father in heaven. It is much better if we can all love one another and forgive and forget. We need to focus on the Bigger Picture. The IMAGE Church of the Church witnesses the community in which we live. Remember my stories that many are watching our witness that we do not know are even watching.

Having issues with the pastor or other church members is not what Jesus would do. He would forgive all as he has forgiven us. Therefore, a non-forgiving spirit by the pastor or a Chuch member is very dangerous. Remember, the Bible teaches us if we do not forgive others, Jesus will not forgive us.

> *Mark 11:25-26: And when ye stand praying, forgive, if ye have anything, against any that your Father who is in heaven may forgive you, your trespasses. V:26: But if ye do not forgive, neither will your Father, who is in heaven forgive your trespasses.*

He wants us to have his type of forgiveness, the kind of forgiveness that can no longer remember an issue that has come between your Christian Brother and us. I am not sure if the Lord can hear our Prayer if we have not forgiven your brother.

No matter your issue with your Church, all should forgive and forget and look at the bigger picture. I pray that all members past, present will unite again in one cause. Forgiving one another as Jesus has forgiven us, that there will be a considerable Home Coming and revival loving one another as Jesus loves us. Remembering there is none of us perfect.

The Bottom Line: the PROMISED LAND IS STILL OPEN TODAY

The fact is the vote to sell the First Baptist Church, built on the Promised Land, in 2013 was reversed. The fact is that there are souls still being saved in it from 1913 until our Lord returns. The truth is that the Chuch is growing, and new missions are being established. Whether you think about past or present members or past or present pastors, past or present church policies, or even if you believe God did not lead me to write this book, you need to focus on the Big Picture. The PROMISED LAND is still thriving and moving forward. God is still blessing the church. I pray that all will come back to worship in the church located on the Promised Land.

Please take the time to go to the new modern website to complete to see what the now renamed Fellowship Church, First Baptist Church located on the Promised Land is doing today. https://www.fellowshipchurch.co/

The Churches new theme in 2020 is the final absolute positive, 100 percent proof to me that those who took a stand to save THE "PROMISED LAND" in 2013 were doing the will of God.

The theme of the church in 2020 is:

"We are one Church gathering in two locations and Three Languages."

This statement on the First Baptist's church website in 2020 tells the whole story that the church is still alive and functioning. It proves that all those who took a stand to save the Promised Land did the right thing, and souls are still saved on the Promised Land because you finished the course and won the race. We did the will of God and the right thing.

This is not the journey's end; it will continue until our Lord returns. I still believe that sometime in the future, the First Baptist Church of Immokalee will do even greater things and experience more extraordinary Miracles. My Lord will use it to do great things for his Glory until he soon returns.

TO GOD BE THE PRAISE AND THE GLORY, AMEND AND AMEND

CPSIA information can be obtained
at www.ICGtesting.com
Printed in the USA
LVHW011032010422
714846LV00006B/9